LOVE SPELLS FOR THE MODERN WITCH

LOVE SPELLS

FOR THE

MODERN WITCH

A SPELL BOOK FOR MATTERS OF THE HEART

MICHAEL HERKES

Illustrations by Studio Muti

ROCKRIDGE
PRESS

Interior and Cover Designer: Regina Stadnik
Art Producer: Janice Ackerman
Editor: Sean Newcott
Production Editor: Rachel Taenzler
Production Manager: Martin Worthington

Illustrations © Studio Muti, 2021

ISBN: Print 978-1-64876-348-9 | eBook 978-1-63807-695-7
R0

To Fiona Horne, for teaching me
how to "Bewitch a Man" many years ago.
Turns out I learned how to bewitch myself
in the process. Hopefully, I can
carry on that tradition to others
with this book.

♥

CONTENTS

INTRODUCTION

I remember it like it was yesterday. The moon was full in the sky, and the room smelled of rose petals and dragon's blood as the smoke from my oil burner swayed in the air. I anxiously scurried to collect all the supplies I could find for a "Come to Me" love spell, dog-eared in *Witch: A Magickal Journey* by Fiona Horne (my favorite book on witchcraft). This was going to be my first spell, and I was obsessing about making sure everything was just right. I was able to find most of the ingredients—pulling two small pink birthday candles from the cupboard, removing seeds from an apple in the fridge, and selecting a pink ribbon I found stashed away in my mom's sewing area. I improvised the rest of the spell's ingredients with what I could find, calling upon what I had read in some other books, including the addition of a red pen and pink piece of paper.

There I sat, by the light of the candles, pouring all of my youthful heart's desires onto the blank page, describing my perfect love. I was lonely and seeking companionship, wanting to experience love just like my friends. Calling out to the Goddess, I asked for a boyfriend as I placed the paper between the two candles, allowing the wax to pour down onto it. Placing the seeds in the paper, I folded it, tying it with ribbon to then be carried with me in my backpack. And just like that . . . my first spell—a love spell—had been cast.

When I started practicing witchcraft 20 years ago, I was in junior high. Hormones were racing, and everyone was getting boyfriends left and right—everyone except for my weird, queer self. Instead, I went inward, soul searching through modern witchcraft. In the beginning, I focused mostly on meditation and moon celebrations—honoring the Goddess and my inner femme force that was surfacing as I came to terms with my sexuality. Sadly, my first spell did not yield the results I had hoped for. Looking back, it was because of the circumstances of my location. To practice magic, you must also make sure that you are actively putting yourself out there in the real world where your spells can work. In my instance, being the only gay kid in the neighborhood did not help my situation.

During my senior year of high school, I had the opportunity to meet witch-author (and now dear friend) Fiona Horne on her book tour for *Bewitch a Man*—an entire book dedicated to love spells. Of course, I was sold. During her lecture on love and spellcasting, she introduced a wonderful mantra to the audience: *"Breathe, Believe, Receive."* Moving forward in my love-witchery, I took a deep breath, relaxed, and continued conjuring my love spells. I believed in their magic, and within months I received my first boyfriend. To my surprise, the spell I had worked years before came true. A carbon copy of the details I'd listed on that piece of paper walked right into my life . . . and in the end it was a dumpster fire of heartbreak. Realizing the power of love magic, I turned to it once again, but this time to heal my sorrow and sadness.

Love can be both beautiful and a hot mess express. While many people turn to magic and witchcraft to manifest the perfect love, magic can get messy, too—not to mention that love spells are a taboo practice that need to be approached with much respect and knowledge.

This book is for those looking to wield their witch power in the palace of love. Part 1 of the book will go over some bewitching basics on how to make love magic and the ethics of spellcasting. I will touch on some historical points, practical magic, correspondences, and "love signs" so that you are well equipped to conjure love for any occasion. Part 2 presents a number of different spells, potions, and rituals to help navigate the many winding roads of love—finding it in yourself, healing from it, protecting against it, attracting it, keeping it, and celebrating it. Regardless of who you are, who you love, how you identify, or even what type of love you are seeking, let us begin witchcrafting your love story with a little bit of magic!

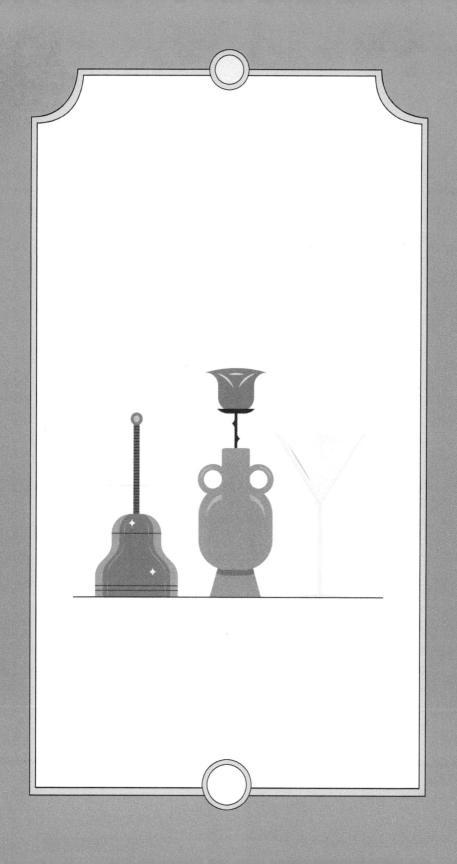

PART ONE

Becoming a Love Witch

Love and witchcraft have been topics of fascination for centuries. In fact, love remains one of the most enticing reasons why people turn to witchcraft, whether to find love, enhance it, repair it, or even end it. You have the power within you to maximize your magical potential and become a love witch, but how do you do it? Where do you begin, and how does it really work? At a basic level, it all comes down to understanding the principal components of love and witchcraft and then merging the two through spellcasting. The next few chapters will serve as a foundation for the witchcrafting discussed in part 2 of this love spell book. Without further ado, let us begin this magical journey—with a shot straight to the heart of it all!

CHAPTER 1

UNDERSTANDING LOVE, MAGIC, AND WITCHCRAFT

L ove is by far the most powerful magic in the universe. All acts of love are magical and provide an abundant supply of energy to tap into. But before diving into the world of love spells, it is important to establish a basic understanding of how and why magic works. The best way to do this is to understand the practical implications of what you are trying to manifest—love. To fully understand love magic, let's go right to the source and look at what love is and why it is so influential.

The Chemistry of Love

Love can be one of the most beautiful experiences that you'll have the pleasure to encounter in life. Whether it be the idea of marriage and children, family and friends, or even the love of your pets, this mysterious emotion is one of the common interests that we share as humans.

Love has been defined in many ways. It is a robust affection for another person, sexual attraction, a warm attachment, an unselfish act of loyalty, a deity, and even a place to thrive in. You have likely been conditioned to believe that your survival is dependent upon resources such as food, water, shelter, and sleep. However, humans also crave connection, both emotional and physical—both of which love serves up on a silver platter.

Your feelings and emotions are the result of chemical reactions in your body. Even though love is typically attributed to your heart, it is actually most connected to two chemicals in your brain: dopamine and oxytocin.

Dopamine is a chemical that helps you feel happiness and pleasure. It is released when you do things that make you feel good—like enjoying delicious food, engaging in exciting activities, and spending time with someone you care about.

Oxytocin, nicknamed the "cuddle hormone," is released in moments of bonding, such as during sex, childbirth, and breastfeeding. In fact, oxytocin is released during skin-to-skin contact between a mother and newborn—resulting in your very first biological connection to love.

Types of Love

Love comes in many forms. The love you have for your partner is much different than that you feel for your mother, your best friend, your mentor, or even yourself. While love can be summed up as a universal emotion and action, it can be broken down into various distinct forms. Realizing that the web love weaves is complex and depends on the situation, the ancient Greeks broke love down into eight varieties:

Agape refers to a spiritual and unconditional love that is selfless in nature and expressed toward everyone. It is also connected to the love felt through compassion and forgiveness—love regardless of flaws, faults, and failures.

Eros is erotic love sparked by primal desire. However, just like a spark, it has a tendency to burn out quickly unless the flame is stoked with other aspects of love.

Ludus is a playful type of love. It is most associated with admiration that leads to innocent teasing, laughter, and warm feelings commonly felt and seen in the "crush" phase of a budding romance.

Mania is a dangerous type of love that defines toxic relationships prone to codependency, jealousy, and violence. The negative actions are a reaction to low self-esteem, which the individual is attempting to compensate for in possessive and venomous ways.

Philautia refers to love and care of the self. It is ingrained in a personal relationship with your own individual needs that further nurtures your self-esteem and confidence. Although this love is focused on the *self*, it has a direct effect on how you interact with and love others.

Philia is the love developed through deep-rooted friendship and affection. It supersedes physical or playful aspects of love in favor of trust, equality, and respect.

Pragma is a mature love that is established through long-standing relationships. It is built on the commitment between individuals that is achieved through honest communication, compromise, and patience.

Storge is the love felt between family members; however, it is not uncommon to see this form of love between friends, coworkers, mentors, and pets. This type of loving bond is established through familiarity and fondness that is developed over time.

LOVE LANGUAGES

In his best-selling book *The Five Love Languages*, author and marriage counselor Gary Chapman details the five ways that love is expressed and received.

1. **Acts of service** are based on doing helpful things for your partner.

2. **Physical touch** is a close physical connection to your partner, such as holding hands, hugging, cuddling, and caressing, as well as sexual intimacy.

3. **Quality time** is all about making the time to show up and be present with your partner.

4. **Gift-giving** is a way of showing your partner that they are on your mind.

5. **Words of affirmation** are verbal reinforcements that demonstrate support of your partner and let them know that you care.

It is from "me" that you can manifest the "we" of a meaningful relationship. One of the best ways to do this is through self-awareness and examining how you like to express and receive love as well as what expressions of love you do not like. For example, let's say you have a partner (romantic or platonic) who is not always around but will continuously tell you how much you mean to them and how grateful they are to have you in their life. If you feel that actions speak louder than words, you may have a primary love language for acts of service and a secondary love language of quality time. Because your partner's way of expressing love with words is different from yours, you may not understand that they are showing love when in fact they are, and vice versa. By understanding the way each of you expresses and wishes to receive love, you will be better equipped to navigate obstacles within your partnership—showing compromise, compassion, and respect for each other's needs.

Having examined the how and why of giving and receiving love, now we can dive into the witchy stuff.

Linking Love and Witchcraft

Have you ever noticed the connection between love and witches in childhood fairy tales? Whether sought after for assistance in attraction, an increase in favorable odds of opportunity, or an antidote to a curse, the labyrinth of love has always been a witch's game.

When things don't work out the way you hoped or you are experiencing an overwhelming obstacle, the idea that you can bend reality to a preferred certainty is a fantastical dream. But the truth is it doesn't have to be a dream, and you don't have to seek out a witch to turn your life into a fairy tale. You can practice magic all on your own.

At their core, witches are practitioners of magic, and magic is the art of creating change with your will. In other words, you manifest your life according to your intentions. For this reason, witchcraft is also a catalyst for creating transformative, positive change in the world—making it a powerful tool for introspection, self-awareness, and personal empowerment. Witchcraft is a means of grabbing your life by the reins and changing course in a favored direction.

One way witches practice magic is by casting spells. A witch's spell is just like a prayer, only performed with a variety of other ingredients that help tip the cosmic scales in your favor for maximum manifestation! Spells are a way of manipulating energy. Everything gives off an energetic output, and witches use objects that correspond to their overall goal in spells to achieve results. Of all the types of spells in the world, none is more coveted than the love spell.

A BRIEF HISTORY OF LOVE SPELLS

Spellcasting has been around for centuries, with the first documented spells dating back to the 5th century BCE in ancient Mesopotamia. Chiseled into stone, the cuneiform incantations featured a variety of magical topics, including–you've got it–love. In those times, love spells were much more extreme, violent, and macabre than they are today, with magical practitioners aiming to "bind" people to their desired outcome.

The majority of love spells have been recorded from Greco-Roman Egypt, where two distinct types were performed: philia, for healing partnerships with affection; and eros, for sexual conquests and domination. Of the two types of love spells, it was more common for women to perform philia spells to inspire affection from their husbands or the head of the household. Love spells would use incantations in jewelry, such as magical necklaces and rings, as well as in knotted cords, brews, and salves, with the aim being to heal anger and build admiration in their partners.

Men primarily practiced eros love spells to provoke lust in the objects of their desire. Whereas the philia love spells were more healing in nature, eros love spells were more similar to curses. In eros spells, the operator would bind images, use animals as sacrifice, and burn items with the hope of dominating their conquest. The victims were often of a young age and still living in their birth homes. The desired goal of the eros spell was to attack their prey with pain and anguish until they left their home and settled in a life with the spellcaster, therefore binding them together.

In medieval England, love potions were created from the internal organs of animals and sweetened for taste with blood and wine. Likewise, records show some spells called for the spellcaster's body hair and fingernails to be crushed into fine powders and added to beverages for their target to drink. A less grotesque practice of love magic from the time was the use of apples for love prophecies, using the peel and other parts to determine someone's future mate.

By the Renaissance period, love spells had become primarily used as a means to obtain marriage, likely because marriage had become a social norm, often established by the class system. Love magic was the preferred means for those less fortunate to gain the admiration of someone of a higher status.

With further regard to gender, love spells and magic have continuously been linked to femininity. Even though both sexes were known to cast love spells in ancient times, prostitutes were mostly associated with love magic because the art of seduction held such power over their conquests. It is from this that the fear of women's sexuality ultimately led to the witch trials. However, it has also been argued that love spells were predominantly cast by men, usually in an attempt to gain the admiration of women who were out of their league.

Regardless, the love spells of the past were mainly built on power and control. One of the most important takeaways from the study of history is, by learning from it, we can evolve and deviate from ancient mistakes. This is why the ethics of spellcasting, particularly with love spells, are so important in modern times.

Ethics of Love Magic

As provocative and intriguing as love spells are, they remain a taboo practice. Some see this form of magic as a manipulative echo of ancient ways of spellcasting—forcing your will on another without their consent. Whereas those spells for love were more controlling in nature, modern witches aim to promote self-love while also attracting a love that is right for them instead of forcing another to love them.

The ethics of love spells, and spellcasting in general, are not a black-and-white approach to determining good versus bad. Take it from Lirio, a magic shop owner in the beloved witch movie *The Craft*, who educates the burgeoning teen witches by stating, "True magic is neither black nor white—it's both because nature is both. Loving and cruel, all at the same time. The only good or bad is in the heart of the witch. Life keeps a balance on its own." Considering this, my recommendation for handling all acts of magic is to ask yourself if *you* think it is okay. If you have any pause regarding a spell—if there is any doubt in your mind telling you that you should not be casting it or that it is wrong—then it is best for you not to continue.

My advice is to instill a good code of ethics into your spellcraft. Working a spell on someone else to get them to love you is not possible, nor would the results be "real" no matter how strong the magic. Even if you were to cast a spell on a specific someone with no interest in you and it worked, the love that they would feel would be artificial. In many cases, magical relationships are doomed from the start because they are built on false love that can ultimately become an act of obsession, and there is a big difference between love and obsession. Love is a universal emotion that is felt equally between partners. Obsession is a self-serving form of mania.

In the end, wouldn't you rather have someone love you for the powerful, gorgeous, badass witch you are than to force them into it? Magic is more than a quick fix for instant gratification. It is always a good thing to focus your love magic efforts on building yourself up to beam with BWE—Big Witch Energy!

Before working a love spell, consider the following five tips:

1. **Identify your true intentions.** Your intentions are both conscious and subconscious. You can tell yourself one thing but really be searching for another. For example, your conscious intention might be for a long-term monogamous relationship, but subconsciously you may be looking for something that is just fun, or you may truly favor a polyamorous relationship. Reflect deeply on what your love goals are—even if your love spells are non-romantic. In a general sense, you have to be prepared for the universe to have a little bit of a say. When you work magic, it is somewhat similar to the magical genie idea where you make a wish and almost get what you asked for—but there is a catch. You may ask for one type of love and get another—the one you *need* rather than the one you *want*. So have a good hard look at what it is that you are looking for—both short term and long term. Do you carry enough love within yourself? Are you caring for your needs and respecting yourself, or are you hoping to complete yourself with another? If the latter, you should really be casting a love spell on yourself.

2. **Do divination.** To assist you in making a decision about whether you should cast a love spell, it is always a good idea to consult divination first. Divination is a practice that helps you see the unseen forces at play and their outcome if you move forward in the manner intended. There are many different ways to practice divination, including reading tarot cards, oracle cards, pendulums, and tea leaves, which will be discussed later in this book.

3. **No consent? No magic!** If you know for a fact that someone is interested in you, then one can argue that doing a spell to pull the two of you closer is ethical. Similarly, if you are in a relationship that has hit rough waters and you are trying to steady your love boat, I believe you are ethically okay to proceed. This is because the person has already established an interest in you and a connection has already been made. You can work with what is already there. However, if the person does not know you

or has explicitly expressed that they are not interested, respect that. Forcing another into an emotional bind with you is magical abuse. Remember, if it feels wrong, it *is* wrong! It is also important to make sure you are not barking up the wrong tree with your love-witchery. No love magic will change someone's orientation. Similarly, it is ill-advised to use love magic to break others up.

4. **Know your stuff.** You will need to have an understanding of the spellcraft you are doing. One of the components of this is educating yourself on the various ingredients and tools used to assist in your spell's manifestation. All of this will be covered in chapter 2, but I encourage you to continue your research with some of the recommended reading provided at the end of the book (see page 160). Spellcasting is serious business. Using the wrong ingredients or going into magic haphazardly is a surefire way to have spells backfire or not work at all. Be respectful of the process.

5. **Do the work.** You have to be practical when you are being magical. For example, if you are working magic to draw love to you, how will you really do that if you are consistently at home watching Netflix? You have to put yourself out there. Think of it this way—if you want to see a dolphin, you have to go to where the dolphins are. You won't see them if you stay on land, nor will you find them in just any body of water. You have to put yourself in the right pool to attract the love you desire. That is the magic of *do*.

LET'S TALK ABOUT HEX

Contrary to popular belief, hexing is not a negative, evil use of magical power—at least it shouldn't be. Instead, consider hexing as nothing more than a spell used to bring justice to an adversarial individual who needs a good cosmic slap in the face. Hexing a toxic ex after a breakup is not only a form of protective magic but also another form of healing. Remember that everything produces energy, and your energy can become intertwined with that of those you love. When they betray or hurt you, causing trauma, you have a right to defend yourself, cut the energetic cord that binds you to them, and call upon the universal forces of justice to help bring closure.

The Healing Power of Love

Aside from calling forth new love or enhancing existing love in relationships, another powerful aspect of love magic is healing. Witches have long been considered healers and are often sought after for magical matters of the heart. Likewise, witchcraft is a personal journey that helps elevate your soul and achieve self-empowerment, which is also a healing act. However, love remains the undercurrent of the healing that witchcraft can provide—to yourself and others.

The highly acclaimed psychiatrist Elisabeth Kübler-Ross has stated that there are only two emotions: love and fear. "All positive emotions come from love, all negative emotions from fear. From love flows happiness, contentment, peace, and joy. From fear comes anger, hate, anxiety, and guilt. It's true that there are only two primary emotions, love and fear. But it's more accurate to say that there is only love or fear, for we cannot feel these two emotions together, at exactly the same time. They're opposites. If we're in fear, we are not in a place of love. When we're in a place of love, we cannot be in a place of fear."

By understanding the power of love and fear, you will be able to understand and take better control of your emotions—healing them on a practical level. Love's emotions can be compacted into states of happiness, empathy, confidence, and acceptance, whereas fear plays out through emotions like anger, abandonment, grief, and shame. Being that they are two sides of the same coin, you can conquer fear-based emotions with an alternative love-based emotion. Denial will cure nothing. The only way out is through—and making the choice to turn a moment of fear into a moment of love is a surefire way of taking responsibility for healing yourself and manifesting happiness.

Just as love and fear cannot exist at the same time, magic and fear also can't coexist. Fear does not provide the clarity to actively and intentionally manifest the positive changes that you are look-ing for in your life. Fear will inevitably be counterproductive to your magical pursuits. But fear will also never go away. It will continue to pop up as you experience new challenges and take yourself out of your comfort zone. However, one of the ways to heal your heart and step out of a state of fear is to choose love.

Looking back, the ancient love spells using philia were cast as a way of healing, to uplift others from anger and fear. One of the best principles of magic is to anchor your spells in ways that enhance the worlds and lives of others. Magic is about being of service. There-fore, looking at love spells as a way to bring positivity to others' lives in addition to your own will always culminate in rich rewards. Similarly, finding compassion within your heart to assist others in need and even to forgive those who have hurt you are powerful ways of practically—and magically—healing with love. Taking time out between relationships to work on yourself is healing with love. Taking the time to grieve and process after the death of a loved one is healing with love. Even hexing a friend's horrible ex who hurt them deeply is an act of healing with love, providing a service for the greater good!

Love, Sex, and Magic

Sex can be an important element of romantic relationships. One of the major reasons I was drawn to witchcraft was its inclusiveness and positive views on sexuality. All acts of love and pleasure are said to be the rituals of the goddess—and witches celebrate this power regardless of gender, orientation, or type of romantic relationship (for example, monogamous versus polyamorous). Today's modern witchcraft has evolved from ancient fertility cults, which saw the commonality in the sacredness of the agricultural land and the reproductive ability of the human body.

Many witches engage in sex magic—the art of using orgasmic energy to fuel a spell or magical working. In the same way that a witch may use the energy of a candle, crystal, or other artifact, orgasms are powerful forces of energy. One of the reasons for this is because your sexuality can create life; it is a creative force that can be harnessed for magical purposes.

When practicing spellcraft with orgasm, you build energy through the potent power of pleasure, and upon the point of climax, you shift your focus and visualize achieving your desired goal. Sex magic can be performed with partners but is most commonly done solo through masturbation. You may incorporate toys, such as the wildly popular crystal Chakrubs, to further amplify the energy you are creating.

Another aspect of sex magic is enhancing your sexual prowess. Whereas eros lust spells from the past were controlling in nature, the best way for modern witches to tap into this primal source of energy is to enchant themselves with lust or the power of seduction to draw potential passion to them.

Coming Out of the Broom Closet

When it comes to matters of the heart, one of the most important steps any magical practitioner must evaluate is whether to come out of the broom closet—or, in other words, whether to disclose that you are a witch to a loved one. As much as witchcraft is booming in popularity these days, there is still a stigma associated with it that can lead to many different types of discrimination. As a result, many witches keep their spiritual and magical practices secret.

Coming out—of any closet—is an extremely personal decision and one that should be gauged based on your surroundings and comfort level. Unfortunately, the world is not always as open-minded as it should be. If you feel as though your well-being is jeopardized by exposing your witchcraft, then you may have good reason to keep it secret.

Dating as a witch can be extremely difficult; however, in my personal experience, it is best to present the information upfront. Being afraid of scaring someone off does not demonstrate the self-love, self-respect, and self-compassion necessary to experience the pure potential of love. It is fear-based emotion that can be more proactively channeled into love. Being honest and open as soon as possible helps reduce the chances of getting rejected once attached. In the past, I waited to reveal who I was, even hiding it for years out of fear of rejection. That said, now I leave the bread crumbs to my gingerbread house of witchiness on my dating profiles. My thinking is: Lead with the most unique qualities that make you who you are . . . how do you stand out in a sea of other fish? Be a witch—be a *love* witch! By understanding both love and witchcraft, you are in a better place to work your magic for any matter of the heart.

Having established the *why* of love-witchery, let us now shift gears to the *how*. In the next chapter, I'll introduce you to the formulary for casting spells and making love . . . magic!

CHAPTER 2

MAKING LOVE . . . MAGIC!

I like to think of spells in the same way that one would about cooking their favorite meal from scratch. It all starts with the trigger of an intention. When you are hungry, you determine what it is that you want to eat. When you are ready to get your witch on, you determine what it is you want to manifest. In both cases, your answer will determine a set of ingredients and a ritual to execute your intention in a way that satisfies your craving. Before you can enjoy the final result, you have to learn how to make the magic happen—how to gather your spell items, use your tools, carry out a ritual, and so on. This chapter is devoted to explaining the methodology of spellcasting and exploring the ingredients you will need to master love magic for any occasion.

Basic Witch Skills

When it comes to practicing magic, it is essential that you understand the basic techniques used in spellcasting. Remember that everything is made up of energy that witches manipulate, direct, and reflect with their will. You are likely familiar with the energy of electricity—but what about magical energy? How does that *feel*? To best get a sense of how energy "feels," try clapping your hands together hard and then rubbing them together vigorously until a pulsing heat forms. Do you notice a tingly pins-and-needles feeling in your skin? That is energy. Now, slowly spread your hands apart so there is about two inches of space between them. With your palms still facing each other, make slow circular movements with each hand, as if you were rotating a tiny ball between your palms. You should feel a slight pressure, similar to that of two magnets trying to push away from each other. Energy is all around you—unseen to the naked eye—and available for you to manipulate. In order to call upon, channel, and direct energy for your spells, I will give you several other techniques to familiarize yourself with before jumping into magic-making.

VISUALIZATION

Visualization is one of the most important parts of spellcasting. The best way to describe the method is to compare it to daydreaming, intently trying to remember a dream you had, or recalling a memory. When daydreaming or recalling a memory, you create a visual story in your mind. When it comes to magic, visualization is a powerful way to further focus and direct your intent. For example, if you are doing a spell to draw love to you, you may visualize yourself covered in a shining light, attracting potential partners to you like moths to a flame, or you may visualize your ideal partner coming into your life. Let's look at two visualization techniques to practice and strengthen your abilities.

Color Breathing

1. In a relaxed state, close your eyes and begin breathing in and out.

2. Pick a color and think about what it means to you.

3. As you breathe in, visualize yourself sucking in the color. In doing so, feel it pour through you, filling you with the feelings you associate with it.

4. As you exhale, push out any unwanted feelings or emotions that contradict the energy of that color.

5. Continue to breathe in and out. As you do, visualize the color getting brighter, deeper, and more vivid.

Room Recall

1. Sit in a relaxed state, closing your eyes and breathing evenly.

2. As you do, imagine yourself in a room that you have been in but presently are not. (One example would be a room in the childhood home where you grew up.)

3. While in the space, take note of the colors, shapes, and art and all visual effects that remain in your memory.

4. Walk around in the room; pick things up. Notice how things feel or even smell.

5. Though this is a memory recall, all of these elements—aesthetics, scent, taste, and feelings—are associated with visualization.

GROUND, CENTER, AND SHIELD

Whereas visualization is the technique of seeing energy, grounding, centering, and shielding are a trio of other techniques commonly used in meditation and energy work. These techniques are used in spellcraft and ritual to set the tone for the magic to follow. They not only prepare you for but also protect you in your magical workings! Much like meditation, these techniques provide you with ways to still your mind and energy in order to establish the mood needed to make magic.

Grounding is the technique of planting yourself in the reality of the moment. Imagine having a busy and hectic day right before you planned to do a spell. Jumping from that chaotic state into a magical state will likely cause your spell to be ineffective or to manifest in an unintended way because your emotions and energy are all over the place. By grounding yourself before spellcasting, you release the weight of the world so that you can be in the right frame of mind for your magic. (It is also important to ground yourself after a spell or magical activity to restore the balance of your mind, body, and spirit.)

How to Ground

1. Sit or stand in a firm position.

2. Close your eyes, breathe in deeply through your nose, and then exhale through your mouth.

3. If you are standing, allow yourself to sink deeply into the ground by pressing your heels down. If you are sitting on the ground, plant your base deeply.

4. Visualize yourself extending into the earth. You may even visualize roots flowing from your body and into the ground.

5. Feel the heavy pull of gravity and a calming sense of stillness.

6. When you feel that your energy is anchored and you have reached a complete state of relaxation, you are ready to move on to centering.

Centering is the ability to reclaim dispelled energy. As you go through your day, you give bits of your energy away—to work, friends, family, partners, and all other obligations. Just like you can't drive a car on an empty tank, practicing magic without energy is going to be a bit tricky. This is where centering comes in handy. By learning to center yourself, you are able to regain an energetic balance, which will be necessary in order to execute your spellcasting with precision.

How to Center

1. After achieving a grounded state of being, close your eyes.

2. Take a deep breath in, feeling your stomach expand. As it does, visualize a ball of light growing from the center of your body.

3. Focus on the ball restoring your energetic output—reclaiming it for yourself.

4. As you exhale and your stomach retracts, visualize the ball growing smaller, releasing any unwanted energy that is blocking your center.

5. Repeat this process until you feel as though your energy is replenished and you are in the right state to begin spellwork.

Shielding is the technique of protecting your energetic input and output. On the one hand, it ensures that negative energy will not penetrate you. On the other hand, it ensures that you are not completely draining yourself in an energetic situation.

How to Shield

1. Just as you did to ground and center, close your eyes and breathe deeply.

2. From the center of your body, visualize a reflective light pouring out over you, forming an energetic sphere around you.

Even though the aforementioned energetic techniques are potent parts of magic, they are also great ways to help manipulate the energy of your everyday life. Creative visualization is a powerful component of manifesting in its own right. Grounding and centering your energy will help you reach a state of relaxation when the going gets rough. Shielding will protect you from negativity while establishing emotional boundaries.

Spell Anatomy

I like to think of spells as the language of magic. They combine the powers of intention, visualization, energy work, and spoken word to result in manifestation. When you perform a spell, it all starts with a purpose and an open mind, followed by a set of actions. Although every spell is different, the formulary of spellcraft can be broken down into the following procedure:

1. **Solidify your goal.** With spellcraft, your will is the key to set your intention free. All forms of magic are reliant upon a purpose to fuel the spell. Ask yourself what it is that you want assistance with. For example, with love spells, what type of love are you trying to manifest? It is worth noting that spells are not a quick-fix bandage for your everyday problems, nor should they be considered an "easy" shortcut to reaching your goals. Magic and spellcraft are serious practices and should be treated as such.

2. **Do the prep work.** Use the laws of attraction to anchor your desires and better guide the universe, your spirit guides, or another form of higher power in bringing you what you want. Remember that everything is composed of energy and combining natural items that correspond to what you are seeking maximizes your spellcasting efforts. For instance, a spell may call for candles of a certain color that connects to your intentions, or maybe it requires a variety of natural energies from sources like crystals, herbs, or essential oils. Be sure to do your research so you know what ingredients are best to use in your spell.

3. **Select the proper timing.** Magical timing is important to use in conjunction with the proper ingredients. I recommend learning about the different days of the week and moon cycles to start with. It is also best to plan to work at a time when you will be undisturbed and in the correct state of mind to perform the spell. For example, jumping right into a love spell immediately after a stressful day of work without first grounding and centering yourself might not be the best option.

4. **Spell it out.** Once you have selected your spell, gathered the ingredients, and determined the right timing, the grand performance is ready to commence. Ground, center, and shield yourself. Declare your intention and perform the necessary actions as outlined in the spell. Be sure to visualize your desired results and speak your spell into the universe. This is why they are called "spells"—you have to *spell out* what you want in order to get what you want!

5. **Take action.** Your spell is only one part of the magic. It is not just about using words, candles, and other witchy items to manifest your desires—you have to couple it with real-world action. After your spell is complete, you need to go after what it is you want. Looking to find new love? You won't find it by isolating yourself at home, so download a dating app and start connecting! Want to bond with friends, family, or a loved one on a deeper level? Make the effort to spend time with them. Want to end a toxic relationship? Come up with a safe and successful exit strategy.

6. **Practice gratitude.** The more you give thanks for what you have and what is coming your way, the more you will become a magnet for an abundance of greatness in your life. If your spell does not appear to be working, don't put negativity into it. Once casting the spell is complete, don't focus on "Is it working? Ugh, I must have messed something up, because it hasn't worked yet!" Have patience—the universe operates on a different understanding of time than you do. Remain positive and grateful.

SPELLCRAFT CONSIDERATIONS

When you are ready to work a spell, there might be additional considerations to think about, depending on what you are doing.

Bathing: This is a great way to cleanse yourself physically and magically before conjuring up your spell. Baths are also magical and can be a spell within themselves!

Clothing: Your wardrobe can greatly enhance your spellcraft. Many witches reserve special outfits for their magic or perform them in the nude, which we call skyclad—being clad only by the sky. Wear clothing that is comfortable and practical for your spellcasting. It might look and feel fabulous to dress in fringe and flowing capes, but if you are walking around a circle of lit candles, you don't want to set yourself on fire!

Eating: As a general rule, it is ill-advised to eat a full meal before a spell. Feeling bloated or uncomfortable will distract from the working.

Location: Work in an environment that is comfortable and where you know you will not be disturbed. This is important for keeping your mind anchored in the intent of your spellcasting. Also, as aesthetically pleasing as it may be to do an evocative ritual in the woods or on a beach, you should always choose a safe location that will not expose you to harm from others, the elements, or animals.

Music: Creating a soundscape can greatly enhance your state of mind for spellcasting. I recommend selecting music or songs that don't adversely distract your working and only add to the energy being manifested—either instrumentally or lyrically.

The Sacred Space

A sacred space is a place that bridges the mundane world and the spiritual plane. It is a state of being that is between the worlds while also in the world of your own source of divinity. There are many natural sacred spaces in the world, such as the historic landmarks Stonehenge and the Great Pyramid of Giza, but they can also be found in the isolated center of a forest or even on the rooftop of a high-rise. Your sacred space is the place that makes you feel your most magical.

ALTARS AND RITUAL TOOLS

One of the best ways to create a sacred space is to make an altar that acts as a focal point for your magical self. In a ritual or spell context, your altar is the place where you meditate and work at the most. Altars and shrines are more than just workstations for spell-craft. They are a reflection of your spirituality. Carving out a space within your home that is devoted to your spiritual path is one way to keep your magic alive and continuously flowing. Altars can hold any kind of spiritual tools necessary for rituals and spellcraft, including the traditional tools of witchcraft:

Athame: A ritual dagger used for directing energy in rituals and spells

Chalice: A ritual cup used for drinking libations or providing offerings

Pentacle: A wooden, clay, or metal disc of the witch's symbol used as a charging plate for magical objects

Wand: An object used to enchant objects; often interchangeable with an athame

Additionally, your altar may include mementos or other artifacts that enrich your practice. Unless you are bound by the rules of a coven or traditional path of witchcraft, you have the freedom to choose how, when, and where you practice in addition to the tools you use in your magic. You do not necessarily need any of the preceding tools to cast spells; however, they can greatly assist your workings if you choose to use them.

Altars can be permanent or temporary, depending on your comfort level and freedoms. Not all spells will require you to work on your altar. That said, I highly recommend creating a space to assist you in shifting your focus for your conjurations.

CASTING A CIRCLE

The circle is an important shape within witchcraft. Many witches perform the act known as "casting a circle," which is an energetically protective ritual for forming a sacred space. A boundary between the realms of the everyday and spiritual planes, a circle acts as an astral church within which to perform spells and rituals. The practice of casting a circle is not always necessary for spellcraft and is more of a personal preference. I typically reserve it for more spiritual acts and worship, like full moon ceremonies or rituals to honor my patron goddess, Lilith. However, if you are new to the craft, this may be a great practice for you to engage in, as it is helpful for centering your mind and grounding your energy during spellwork. An important feature of circles is that they encompass all of the four elements—earth, air, fire, and water—so be sure to have a representation of each (i.e., crystal or rock salt for earth, incense stick or feather for air, candle for fire, and bowl of water or seashells for water). Although there are many resources out there that detail how to cast a circle, including my previous books (see Recommended Reading on page 160), here is a general overview of the process:

1. Begin by purifying the area. This can be accomplished by burning incense or a smudge stick, ringing a bell, or mixing sea salt in purified water and sprinkling it around the space. Purification removes any unwanted energies and prepares the space for ritual.

2. Gather your supplies and set up your space. Ground yourself and center your mind to begin the spell.

3. Combining visualization with movement, cast your circle by holding out your index finger (or a ceremonial tool such as an athame or wand, if available) and walking the perimeter of your circle in a clockwise direction while saying:

> *I call upon the magic circle,*
> *a circle outside of time and place,*
> *to house the magic I conjure.*

While doing this, visualize a stream of light pouring out from your finger or tool and forming a sphere around your space.

4. Call the elements/quarters by inviting each element into your space with its corresponding direction (earth/north, air/east, fire/south, water/west) in the same clockwise fashion. You can call them in by saying:

> *I call upon the power of (element name)*
> *in the (direction)*
> *and ask that you aid in my magical working.*

5. If deities or ancestors are an integral part of the working, invite them into the circle by calling upon them.

6. Declare your intention and perform the spell.

7. Raise energy by chanting, singing, dancing, or performing any other activity that stirs up power and excitement.

8. Ground and center yourself again. In traditional rituals, this is done with food and/or a libation that connects to the spell.

9. Release the ritual by expressing gratitude to the deities, universe, and/or your version of a higher power.

10. Thank the elements at each corresponding cardinal direction, moving counterclockwise.

11. Release the circle by moving counterclockwise and declaring:

> *This circle is open, but unbroken, carried forever with*
> *me in my heart.*

Correspondences for Love Magic

Now that you have an understanding of how to work love magic, let's look at some of the specifics you can use to manifest your heart's desire. This section is composed of the various correspondents necessary for making your love magic, including magical days, moon cycles, colors, herbs, crystals, and other ingredients.

DAYS OF THE WEEK

Each day of the week is ruled by a planet, providing a celestial energy source to tap into for your spellcasting. Of all the days of the week, Friday is most associated with love magic; however, the other days of the week can always provide additional layers to your love spells.

Monday: Ruled by the moon, Monday is associated with intuition and femininity. It is a great day to do spells that speak to wisdom in love.

Tuesday: Ruled by Mars, love spells are best performed on Tuesday for results tied to passion and sex.

Wednesday: Ruled by Mercury, the planet of communication, this is a great day to do love spells to enhance communication in relationships as well as spells that aid in compromise and self-expression.

Thursday: Ruled by Jupiter, this day is great for expansion, abundance, and luck. It is a great day to do spells for love associated with longevity, entering new phases of relationships, and luck in love.

Friday: Ruled by Venus, this day is an all-around lovefest! It is a blanket day for love as it is connected to Venus/Aphrodite, the Greek goddess of love, and named after the Norse goddess of love, Freya.

Saturday: Ruled by Saturn, this is a good day to clear negativity and break ties with toxic or unwanted love.

Sunday: Ruled by the sun, Sunday is a great day for overall success and wishes within love. It is also a good day to work with masculine solar energies.

TO VENUS AND BACK

When working love magic, it is very important to have an understanding of the planet of love–Venus! Named after the Roman goddess of the same name, Venus is the planet associated with love, beauty, and money. When you are working out your magical timing by the days of the week, I encourage you to work during the planetary hour of Venus for all love spells. This will only magnify and intensify your magic and add further fuel to the flames of the love you are conjuring. To determine the planetary hour of Venus based on your geographical location, check out Astrology.com .tr/planetary-hours.asp. It is also recommended not to work love magic during Venus retrograde–a period where the planet appears to move backward. During this time, all matters of the heart can feel stagnant, causing challenging emotions.

MOON PHASES

The moon is deeply tied to witchcraft. Although it's not always necessary to work with the moon, it can assist with providing an additional layer of energy for timing your spells.

New moon: Great for planting the seed of love, the new moon is a good time to work spells that open the door to finding new love and opportunities in your life.

Waxing moon: The waxing moon is the time between the new and full moons and is divided into three parts: waxing crescent, first quarter, and waxing gibbous. The waxing phase of the moon is a good time to do spells for attracting things and situations to you as well as for taking action, making decisions, and getting specific about what type of love you want to bring into your life.

Full moon: The full moon is seen as a time to work any type of magic since the lunar essence is at its peak. Often a time to celebrate lunar energies, the full moon is a great time to reflect and rejoice in your magical endeavors.

Waning moon: The waning moon is the time between the full and new moons and is divided into three parts: waning gibbous, third quarter, and waning crescent. Overall, the waning moon phases are a time to release and let go of what is no longer serving you in addition to practicing gratitude for what you have done spellcasting for.

Eclipses: Some witches choose not to do any spellwork during eclipses due to the lingering ideology that they are "bad." In ancient times, eclipses were considered frightening episodes, and many cultures saw them as the representation of malevolence. That said, eclipses are an extremely potent time to work magic, because they combine solar and lunar energy, making for an extremely powerful event to draw from.

You don't have to completely hold out on performing a spell if its goal does not align perfectly with the phase. For example, let's say you want to cast a spell to bring love to you, but it's the waning moon. You can change the wording of your spell so that instead of trying to attract during a time for release, you release the obstacles standing in your way, thereby better allowing love to come to you.

Additionally, the moon enters a new zodiac sign every two to three days. To determine which sign the moon is in, you can refer to Mooncalendar.astro-seek.com. The moons most associated with love are:

Moon in Aries and Scorpio: Sex and passion

Moon in Taurus and Libra: Sensual love and romance

Moon in Cancer: Family matters

Moon in Leo: Self-love and confidence

For a more detailed look at moon magic, check out my book *The Complete Book of Moon Spells*!

LOVE DEITIES

Since the dawn of time, civilizations have prayed to a number of different deities for assistance in all areas of their lives. Love has always been one of the leading areas of life for which deities have been sought out. Many witches work with various pantheons and deities for assistance in their spellwork. If you choose to do so, I recommend conducting some research on the entity you are calling upon to understand their preferred offerings and means of contact. When working with any deity, remember to be respectful and polite; you are coming to them for assistance and should treat them accordingly. The following are some of my favorite goddesses and gods of love and sexuality from around the world, including the specific types of love that they speak to and can help you work with:

Aphrodite/Venus (Greek/Roman): Love, passion, desire, joy, beauty

Cernunnos (Celtic): Fertility, sex, lust

Dionysus (Greek): Marriage, ecstasy, madness

Eros/Cupid (Greek/Roman): Love, passion, desire

Erzulie (Vodou): Love, beauty, passion, prosperity

Freya (Norse): Love, beauty, war

Hathor (Egyptian): Love, fertility

Hera/Juno (Greek/Roman): Love, marriage

Inanna/Ishtar/Astarte (Sumerian/Babylonian/Phoenician): Love, war, sex, beauty

Isis (Egyptian): Eternal love

Lilith (Sumerian/Hebrew): Lust, sex, self-love, equality, divorce

Oshun (Yoruban): Love, passion, sensuality

Osiris (Egyptian): Eternal love

Pan (Greek): Lust, sex

Tu'er Shen (Chinese): Homosexual love

Yemaya (Yoruban): Love, fertility, sensuality

Just like physical items of the natural world, symbols are imbued with their own powerful energy. Symbols can be carved into candles or drawn on other spell ingredients to further define a spell's purpose.

IMAGE	SYMBOL	MEANING
	ANKH	Egyptian symbol of life and immortality; also used to represent fertility and the sexual union of male and female.
	APPLE	A popular symbol of love and wisdom; also represents fruitful relationships. Referenced in many mythologies, such as the Garden of Eden and the story of Venus, the Roman goddess of love.
	CLADDAGH	Irish love symbol and common ring design; combines the heart to represent love, the hands for friendship, and the crown for loyalty.
	COPPER ALCHEMY SYMBOL	Associated with Venus, the planet of love.
	CUPID'S HEART	A symbol for the god of love. It represents the attraction of love.
	DOVES AND SWANS	Symbolic representations of love and associated with the goddess Aphrodite/Venus. Known for their monogamous mating habits, they thus symbolize long-lasting true love.
	HEART	The universal symbol for love.
	KNOTS	Knots represent the combined infinite union of partnership. Handfasting, a witch's marriage ritual, uses knotted cords to represent the joining of two lovers.
	ROSE	Most popular floral symbol of love. Different colors of roses can represent different types of love: white = divine love, yellow = friendship, pink = romance, red = romantic love.
	SHELLS	A popular symbol of love due to Aphrodite/Venus being portrayed standing in a giant scallop shell in Botticelli's famous painting *The Birth of Venus*.

Making Love . . . Magic!   **35**

GENDER SYMBOLS	The gender symbols are also the symbols for Venus (female; circle resting on top of cross) and Mars (male; arrow coming from side of circle). The symbols can be combined to represent a variety of gender and romantic partnership combinations (male + female = heterosexual, male + male = gay, female + female = lesbian, etc.).
	Gay couple
	Heterosexual couple
	Lesbian couple
	Polyamory (any combination of three or more gender symbols)
	Transgender

CANDLES FOR LOVE

Candles are powered by the element of fire—an agent of transformation, change, and sensuality. Witches see power in the energy of color because every color has its own unique energetic vibration that can greatly impact magic. Although most of the time love is associated with colors like red or pink, other colors can also add elements of power to any love working.

Red: Romantic love, lust, sexuality

Pink: Self-love, compassion, emotional healing

Orange: Confidence, courage, creativity

Yellow: Friendship, happiness, success

Green: Fertility, marriage, prosperity

Blue: Peace, communication, fidelity

Purple: Spirituality, soul mates, wisdom

Black: Banishing, endings, protection

Brown: Grounding, happy home, stability

White: Serenity, peace, all-purpose (except banishing!)

PLANTS FOR LOVE

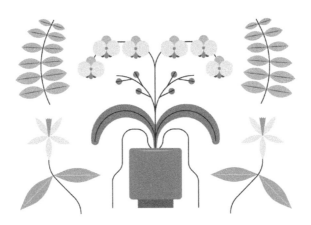

Because witchcraft is so deeply connected to nature, plants are one of the main sources of energy used in magic. Fresh or dried plants may be mixed into powders for incense, rubbed on candles, or placed inside other magical items. Essential oils are also extracted from leaves, flowers, and fruits to then be used to anoint, or apply on, various magical objects in spellcraft or blended into fragrances. However, floral oils like rose and jasmine, which are major staples of love magic, can cost hundreds of dollars. My recommendation is to find a good-smelling synthetic oil and then add pieces of the corresponding dried herb. For example, adding dried rosebuds or petals to rose oil will help infuse the oil with the plant's natural properties.

There are many different plants that can be used in love spells. Some of the more common ones include:

Apple: Promotes knowledge and wisdom in love

Basil: Aids in good fortune and familial love and is perfect for love spells for those you share a home with

Cardamom: Stimulates lust and sexual energy

Carnation: Attracts loving friendships and can be used to deepen love in existing relationships

Catnip: Attracts love with excitement

Chile pepper: Can be used for love-related protection and justice

Chocolate: Stimulates excitement and attracts love

Cinnamon: Used to promote luck in love and enhance sexuality

Clary sage: A euphoric aphrodisiac that produces healing energy and balance while also boosting sensuality

Clove: Attracts love and stimulates self-confidence

Damiana: A known aphrodisiac and classic ingredient for love and lust spells

Dragon's blood: Used in love spells related to relationship longevity and good for marriage and proposals

Ginger: Attracts love and promotes confidence within love

Hibiscus: Stimulates sexuality and deep romantic love

Hyacinth: A powerful flower of love, especially for homosexual relationships

Jasmine: A classic floral ingredient for love spells that is great for enchantment and sensual love

Lavender: Promotes calming and tranquil love

Lemon: Used to cleanse and purify love

Lily: A powerful flower for lust that can also be used to end relationships

Lovage: Great for strengthening or reviving love

Orchid: A great flower to use for self-love and independence, as orchid roots can be used to strengthen and harmonize existing relationships

Orris root: Helps draw true love to you

Patchouli: A pungent-smelling herb that stimulates sexy attractiveness

Rose: A classic flower for all shades of love. Buds are wonderful for new romance, while a full bloom symbolizes established romance. A thorny stem can assist with protection and breakups.

Strawberry: Attracts good fortune in love and fertility

Vanilla: Can be used to sweeten love. As an aphrodisiac, it can be used to stimulate lust.

Ylang-ylang: A soothingly sensual fragrance that promotes confidence

Holding an abundance of natural earth energy, crystals are used in spells to amplify energy and intentions. They can be worn as jewelry, added to spell bags, held during meditations, or arranged in geometric grids around other objects to help intensify the magical energy you are calling upon. Additionally, they can be used to cleanse or charge an item in preparation for magical use. There are hundreds of different crystals in the world, many of which emulate the energy of love. Some favorites that I would recommend for your spellwork include:

Amethyst: Assists in making wise decisions when it comes to matters of the heart

Aventurine: Encourages mature love

Carnelian: Helps instill confidence and sexual desire

Clear quartz: Amplifies all energy

Diamond: The most popular stone for wedding bands, diamonds are a source of purity and strength in love

Emerald: Associated with the heart chakra, this crystal promotes healing with love while strengthening relationships and encouraging faithfulness

Garnet: Perfect for passion and sexual desire

Herkimer diamond: Has a crystal memory that can be instilled with vibrations and memories of love

Jade: An all-encompassing love stone that also supports fidelity

Kunzite: Helps instill positive communication in partners

Lodestone: A magnetized mineral that is used to attract love to you

Malachite: Encourages healthy, loving relationships

Moonstone: Brings new beginnings and good fortune in love

Morganite: Helps promote an abundance of love energy

Pink opal: A great loving stone that helps bring acceptance, reconciliation, and resolution to matters of the heart

Pink tourmaline: Helps heal stress and anxiety

Rhodochrosite: Helps draw true love to you while healing from past wounds and not making the same mistakes; a great stone for self-love and happiness

Rhodonite: Helps restore balance in loving relationships and remove codependency; good for self-love

Rose quartz: Classic love stone that assists in instilling compassion and affection

Ruby: Increases and intensifies love and sexual relationships

Thulite: Helps you heal from abuse and provides the strength to exit toxic relationships

Topaz: Attracts genuine love and provides good fortune in all matters of the heart

Twin quartz: A special formation where two crystals form from the same base; great for relationships and finding your soul mate

EMPOWERING YOUR INGREDIENTS

Before casting any spell, it is a good idea to cleanse and empower your ingredients. Doing so helps remove any negativity that may be attached to them while also telling them what their purpose is for the spell.

1. Close your eyes and take a few deep breaths.

2. Taking hold of your gathered supplies, visualize a light pouring from your hands and into the objects.

3. As you do, lightly breathe onto them and say something along the lines of:

   With the power of my will, I cleanse you of any negativity and ask that you aid me in my magical working for (type of magic—in our case, "love").

GENERAL EQUIPMENT

In addition to the ingredients discussed so far, there are a few standard pieces of equipment that you should have on hand for spellwork:

Bottles and containers to hold leftover ingredients; it's good to have a few different sizes available

Carrier oils like jojoba oil or fractionated coconut oil to dilute harsh essential oils and stretch them out

Drinking glasses for edible elixirs

Fireproof bowl for burning ingredients

Incense holder for burning incense

Knife for cutting herbs and carving candles

Matches/lighter for lighting candles

Measuring bowls and spoons to properly calculate the amount of ingredients called for

Mixing bowls to hold liquids, herbs, and powders

Mortar and pestle for grinding herbs

Saucepans for brewing potions

Modifying and Creating Your Own Spells

Chances are that as you move through life and a myriad of love-related situations, you may not find a spell that's just right for the occasion. This is common with any type of spellcraft and is nothing to fret over! Whenever you are in a bind or your resources are limited, you can always modify spells according to your needs.

The biggest thing you need to do in these instances is pay attention to your magical correspondences (i.e., colors, crystals, herbs, etc.). For example, though you can swap out sugar and use stevia for a cooking recipe, if you swapped sugar with salt, you wouldn't get the right result for the meal (and also . . . yuck!). The same is true with magical ingredients. A magical misapprehension that I have seen sprout up from time to time is the idea that spellcraft is *only* about intention and that whatever you feel will work *will* work because it is your intent for it to work. For example, "My intuition told me to use a black candle and peppercorns for this love spell, so I did." But it does not work like that—black is for banishing and pepper is for protection, so what you really did was build a magical wall around yourself, protecting you from romantic advancements when you were hoping to have suitors calling. Look for what gives off the same energy you are looking for. If you are a performing a spell meant to bring love to you, you can generally substitute a rose for any other flower that stimulates love energy. You may also choose not to even use an ingredient—and that is acceptable, too.

Additionally, you may realize that you need more ingredients. For example, a couple may be looking to become a *throuple* (a romantic relationship between three people), so a basic come-to-me love spell can be modified to a come-to-*us* love spell with some adjustments of words—and maybe an extra candle or crystal. Some potions may be alcohol-based but can easily be made nonalcoholic by swapping out spirits with iced tea. (Note: Use white teas for clear liquor and black teas for dark.) The spells that I have included in part 2 of the book should be easy to modify if necessary, and I will do my best to provide alternatives for any items that may be a bit more obscure or hard to find.

Any witch will tell you that the most effective spells you will ever cast are those that you create yourself. Spells do not have to rhyme like you often see in TV and movies; however, rhyming is a great tool to use for memorization, and I personally love to follow this method in my spellwork. Memorization can pack a powerful punch of emotional connection, similar to an actor/actress committing to their lines. If you have writer's block and are unable to think of the "write" words, one trick I use for inspiration is the lyrics from some of my favorite songs, which should be exceedingly easy when it comes to love. You can even play love songs in the background during your spellwork to add an extra oomph of energy! So tweak, tailor, and create your own spells as you see fit—just always be responsible with your choices.

Learning the fundamental components of magic is a necessary part of successful spellcasting. Having looked at the *how*, you are one step closer to casting love spells. But you have one more stop on your love magic journey before you can start practicing spell-craft. Pack your bags and grab your broomsticks—we are heading to the stars to understand the cosmology of love astrology!

CHAPTER 3

LOVE AND COSMIC COMPATIBILITY

One of the oldest pickup lines used to court potential lovers is "What's your sign?" In today's modern culture of witchery, the question has evolved even further into asking "What time were you born?" Although astrology is an area of focus for many witches, it is also a common area of curiosity for others outside the magical community. Whether proudly displayed on the body in the form of tattoos, the topic of choice over coffee and cocktails, or the inexhaustible subject of online quizzes, astrology is continuously used as a tool to determine compatibility with lovers, friends, family members, and even coworkers. This chapter will explore the all-encompassing power of love through a natal chart. By understanding your star signs and when the stars align, you can look deeper into the cosmic compatibility of all your relationships.

Witchcraft and Astrology

The stars and cosmos have been considered a symbolic language that was first established by the ancient Babylonians, who saw the celestial marvels as mirrors into the personalities and destinies of humans. In modern witchcraft, astrological and planetary attributions are often applied to the aspects of magical timing, herbalism, crystals, colors, and compatibility that we touched on in chapter 2 (page 19). Astrological symbols can be carved into candles or drawn on other magical objects to help attract a compatible mate to you or even help heal the bond of an existing partnership. Therefore, having an understanding of cosmic compatibility adds another energetic layer to your love spells.

Understanding Your Natal Chart

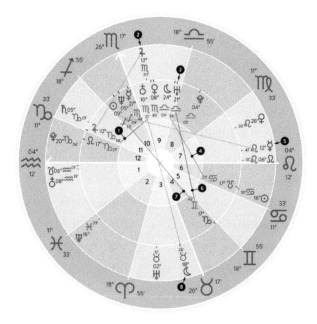

In astrology, a natal chart is a visual diagram that maps the exact positions of the sun, moon, and other planets at the time of your birth. When you look at a natal chart, it is really a celestial blueprint for your life—highlighting the various layers of your personality and destiny. There are many different sources available to find your natal chart online, and if you have never done so, I recommend generating one for free on Astro.com. You will need to know your date, time, and location of birth to get the most accurate results. If you don't have access to some of this information, such as your exact time of birth, do your best to enter the information that you know to be true. Most generators will include an "unknown" option that will at least give you some idea of the potential chart.

It is very common for people to explore astrological compatibility between different zodiac signs. But determining your compatibility is more than just figuring out your sun sign, or the typical zodiac sign that you'll see at the back of newspapers and magazines. There are many different components at play. If you happen to read tarot, you know that when a spread is drawn, the cards each carry their own significant themes and meanings, and in order to effectively read the spread, you must consider the meaning of each card within the context of the surrounding cards. Although it may be tempting, you cannot solely focus on the card that represents the future, or the final outcome. It is similar to the age-old saying "greater than the sum of our parts"—it doesn't solely matter what an individual tarot card or zodiac sign is, because when looked at as a whole, their meanings add up in a different way.

There are many different planets and asteroids that make up your natal chart—each with its own unique energetic meaning that influences you. To better break it down, let us explore the various "signs" and how they relate back to compatibility and partnership.

SUN SIGN

When you are asked, "What's your sign?" the most common answer given is your sun sign. This is the zodiac sign that the sun was in during the time of your birth. It is the representation of your identity and helps illustrate who you are in this life on an external level.

Because of this, it is given the most significance in the mainstream world, and although certain identities are more harmonious than others, your emotions, along with elements such as communication, aggression, and love languages, are further fleshed out through other signs that were present at your time of birth.

MOON SIGN

Your moon sign is the representation of your emotional landscape. Whereas the sun sign represents your external personality, your moon sign represents your inner mood and temperament. Because love is such a strong emotion, your moon sign will help you better understand how you process your feelings for others and what you need to feel emotionally safe and secure in relationships.

RISING SIGN

Your rising sign (sometimes called your ascendant) rules over your social personality. Sometimes considered the "mask" you show the world, this sign is the first impression you give others—like a book cover awaiting judgment. This includes how you carry yourself, how you interact with others, how you dress, and the overall way that others perceive your attitude.

MERCURY SIGN

The way you express yourself with your words can have a real effect on how others perceive you as well as how you take in and absorb information from those around you. The planet Mercury represents communication styles: how we think, write, speak, learn, and share information with others. Because communication is so essential to any relationship, your Mercury sign is very much at play for determining compatibility.

VENUS SIGN

This sign indicates your value of love, beauty, aesthetics, and finances. Considered the love sign, it showcases how you give and accept love and provides insight into your preferred and chosen love languages. Understanding your Venus sign will provide a deeper level of understanding when it comes to determining your romantic compatibility with others.

MARS SIGN

Mars is the planet of war, and in the context of your natal chart, it indicates your passions, level of courage, sense of confidence, sexual impulses, and disagreement style. The sign can provide a better understanding of how you communicate in general through your Mercury sign in times of anger and frustration, and it also adds an extra layer of understanding to how you express yourself sexually in romantic relationships alongside your Venus sign.

ELEMENTAL SIGNS

The twelve signs are divided into four elemental aspects that can help in identifying and understanding their nature. The characteristics of the element help shed light on the demeanor of the signs. As a general rule, air and fire signs are considered more compatible, whereas earth and water signs are better suited for each other.

Earth signs (Taurus, Virgo, Capricorn): Grounded and analytical

Air signs (Gemini, Libra, Aquarius): Creative and social

Fire signs (Aries, Leo, Sagittarius): Ambitious and full of energy

Water signs (Cancer, Scorpio, Pisces): Imaginative and dreamy

Understanding the Signs

The following descriptions provide a blanket overview of the zodiac signs, regardless of their planetary placement. Look at these signs as the players, with the previous planetary associations representing the stage on which they act out their lives. Although each planetary association plays out a little differently, I have included keywords at the end of this section to help in understanding the dominant trait of each planet. For example, a Venus in Cancer is going to express themselves as a Cancer when it comes to matters of the heart, beauty, and finance.

ARIES

As the first sign of the zodiac, Aries are feisty fire signs that are full of life. They are pure energy and crave adventure. They are the doers and enjoy others who appreciate their high-octane personalities and energy level. In romantic love and sex, Aries brings the heat—loving hard and falling fast. Though often independent, the full-of-life and adventure-seeking Aries are extremely social and like to immerse themselves in various activities, making their relationships to family and friends exciting. In work, Aries are ambitious and creative leaders. Due to their fast-paced nature, they tend to excel in positions that require changing priorities. When working with an Aries, try not to pin them down or push them into monotonous work. They need freedom and variety as well as opportunities to lead and take charge. When it comes to navigating the landscape of someone with an Aries sign, avoid confrontation, as this sign is known for having a knee-jerk reaction to their emotions and explosive tempers. This sign tends to be more cerebral in that they can lack the empathy needed to ascertain others' emotional needs during conflict. In all relationships, Aries must balance "me" and "we" and understand that there is no "I" in "team."

TAURUS

Ruled by the planet Venus, Taurus is one of the most loving signs and has a deep appreciation for comfort—be it cozy snuggles, affection, luxurious items, or food. In romantic partnerships they love deeply and sensuously. This sign is down to earth and goes with the flow. However, because of their "bullheaded" nature, they can often struggle with compromise. With friends and family, Taurus tends to be a grounding force that offers stability for those who care about them. When it comes to career, they excel in jobs that provide routine. As a fixed earth sign, Taurus is like a mighty mountain—meaning it is an extremely stubborn sign that does not react well to being pushed into anything. They do not like change. Those who are interacting with someone with Taurean qualities do best at coaxing the bull with what it loves most—comfort and food—rather than trying to push them into a situation that is outside their comfort zone. Taurus is also known for being extremely possessive, having an almost materialistic view of others in their life. Taurus's major lesson in relationships is to lead with their warm heart and learn the art of being open-minded.

GEMINI

Gemini is an air sign ruled by communicative Mercury. Known as the sign of the "twins," Geminis can be a bit of a flip-flop personality, changing course at any given moment. Because of this, they are also often labeled as the Dr. Jekyll and Mr. Hyde sign of the zodiac—bouncing between harmonious and explosive expressions of emotion. But duality is the nature of this sign, not equality. In romance, Geminis are always up for new adventures and seek partnership with those who want to have fun. Good communication and loyalty are two areas they want in any relationships—romantic, familial, or platonic. On a career level, Geminis excel in roles where they are able to flex communication skills, such as journalism, marketing, and the arts. Any project that requires documenting procedures and explaining processes works best for them, and they love mentoring novices. When one or more of your signs is in Gemini, communication is a major part of your planetary alignment. Those interacting with someone who has Gemini placements must remain cognizant that communication is the key to unlocking their heart. A Gemini's greatest lesson is that not everyone interacts the way they do, and at times silence is the best form of communication.

CANCER

Cancer is a water sign ruled by the moon and is extremely receptive to emotions. This vulnerable sign is full of emotion and has a great need for safety and security in all things. Because of this, their relationships are built upon loyalty and trust. Since they are vulnerable, they find comfort in their emotional landscape and may push away—feeling more comfortable in their own shell than openly expressing their feelings. Romantically, Cancers are extremely loyal and express their love through romance and affection. Family and friends are major factors in their lives. Cancers are extremely supportive of others and always want to be of service to those they care about. This parental nature gives them a strong work ethic in careers where they can support others. Because of their emotional nature, Cancers can be a bit moody, clingy, and suspicious. The best way to work with Cancers is to be as supportive of them as they are of you, if not more so. Cancer's biggest challenge in partnerships is practicing self-care and focusing on their needs over obligations to others. It's all about balance.

LEO

Leos are the fiery actors of the zodiac. They have a flair for the dramatic and live for the independence and freedom of a wild feline. Their courageous personalities make them well liked by many, but their exuberance can sometimes be off-putting to more introverted individuals. In romance they are bold and forward—often known for making grand gestures when courting a new flame. When it comes to family and friends, Leos are very protective of their loved ones. Like other fire signs, Leos excel in leadership roles and have a high drive for ambitious career initiatives. They love lots of feedback that makes them feel valued and wanted—in all areas of their life. They are a star in their own mind and want recognition for that. Leo's biggest challenge in partnerships is to understand that they are not always the starring role and that relationships built on equality have the best outcomes.

VIRGO

Virgo is an observant and dependable earth sign. Ruled by Mercury—the planet associated with how we process information—they genuinely want to fully understand everything there is to know about someone they care for. Having a strong loyalty for those they love, they are always there for their romantic partners, friends, and family. However, Virgos tend to be more expressive through their actions rather than providing verbal affection and appreciation. Well organized and dedicated, they excel in jobs that offer structure and reliability. Any position that allows them to fully express their organization skills is preferred. It goes without saying that they generally have an adverse reaction to disorganization and chaotic environments. They are also known for being judgmental and lean on the side of perfectionism—projecting unrealistic expectations onto others. Virgos may come off as shy in the beginning, but it is only because their analytical nature likes to take everything in before they feel comfortable engaging. Virgos do well with those who are reliable and provide stability in their lives. Although they love order and want things to be "perfect," a Virgo's biggest lesson is to embrace the unknown and go with the flow.

LIBRA

The second sign ruled by Venus, Libra is a charming air sign that values love, harmony, and equality. Known for being a sign based on equality and justice, Libras are also masters of beauty and romance. All forms of partnership are very important to Libras. As a Venusian sign, they also like to surround themselves with the luxuries of art, fashion, and fine dining. They make great lovers who are open to compromise and like to examine their emotions in relation to how others feel. Because of this, they are often a neutral party in chaotic situations and assist their friends and family by always being someone to offer great advice. In their careers, they prefer anything that is harmonious and excel in positions that promote justice or beauty, typically in lawful or artistic roles. Those interacting with Libras will find that their harmonious nature makes them one of the easiest signs to get along with—avoiding all confrontation and conflict. Libras are represented by the scales because they tend to be indecisive—continuously weighing all of their options. This can sometimes cause them to tolerate negative situations for longer than they should. A Libra's main lesson is to trust their intuition when it comes to making decisions and establish boundaries with that which does not serve them.

SCORPIO

Dark and mysterious, this water sign is ruled by both Mars and Pluto, making it well versed in the areas of anger, sexuality, and death. Scorpios are deeply passionate and sensual lovers with a hypnotic sex appeal and flirtatious demeanor. They love the chase or courting and have a flair for the dramatic. Displaying courageous confidence, their magnetic personalities make them a very attractive sign. However, they are deeply intuitive and prone to overthinking and jealousy. They tend to hold a lot of their emotions in and viciously attack others when they feel as though their boundaries have been crossed. For this reason, they are often skeptical of romantic relationships. They are loyal, authentic, and honest in their friendships and family, always there to provide the truth to any situation—usually with a splash of humor. In work and finance, Scorpios are very disciplined and analytical, making them well suited for managing projects and a variety of tasks. They excel in work environments where they have respect for those they work with and for. Scorpio's biggest lesson is to release paranoia and embrace vulnerability. It's best to be honest and up front in all inter-actions with Scorpios.

SAGITTARIUS

Another fire sign, Sagittarius is adaptable and loves change and transformation. Ruled by Jupiter, Sags enjoy philosophical and spiritual studies, perception, and travel. This sign loves freedom—especially when it comes to mental pursuits. Like the other fire signs, they are very energetic and engaging, making them great lovers. They are charming and particularly love partnerships that flex their intellectual and spiritual curiosity. In their friendships and family matters, they bring a warm sense of optimism that makes others feel cared for and appreciated. Considering their interests, Sags work best when they can learn from or mentor others—making them great teachers, tour guides, and planners. However, those who are interacting with Sag placements must understand that they do not like confinement and need an open space to let their fiery passions blaze. They also are known for feeling restless and wanting to run free, which can cause them to cut ties with others more easily than most. Their reckless behaviors can sometimes get them in trouble. Their biggest lesson in relationships is to think before they act.

CAPRICORN

Capricorn is a cardinal earth sign ruled by Saturn, planet of discipline and responsibility. They tend to prefer traditional paths and have a strong sense of societal expectations. In love relationships, Capricorns are very stubborn and hard to get. They do not give their love easily, but once they do, they are extremely loyal. Within their family and friendship dynamics, Capricorns are the self-appointed leaders. This drive for leadership, coupled with supreme organization skills, makes Capricorns excel in work environments where they can be the boss. They are sometimes known for being obsessive about their careers and the legacy that they will leave behind. Those who engage with Capricorn placements must be understanding of their priorities. Because their value system is built around going after what they want at any cost, they appreciate anyone with a strong sense of dignity and work ethic—not just when it comes to career. Capricorns have a tendency to over-romanticize the way in which the outside world sees them, putting a lot of pressure on themselves. Their biggest lesson is to accept themselves. Only then can they experience the secret to success—their happiness.

AQUARIUS

The air sign Aquarius is known for being one of the most bizarre in the zodiac—in the best way possible! This sign has been called the most alien of the zodiac signs due to their extreme independence, rebellious nature, and fascination with technological features—always looking to deviate from the status quo in favor of innovative new ideas. Because of this, they easily make new friends while also being seen as major outcasts. In all relationships, they can come off as detached from human emotion, often focusing on the achievement of perfection. Nevertheless, when they fully commit to a romantic relationship, they are uniquely passionate. Because air signs rule over communication, Aquarians are incredibly social, with a deep love for bringing others together. In work, their independent natures make them wonderful entrepreneurs, and they excel in positions that provide service to others. Those who are dealing with Aquarius positions should understand that this unique sign must march to the beat of their own drum and that confining actions or viewpoints will not work for them. Their biggest lesson in relationships is to remain uniquely independent while also remembering that emotions are a two-way street.

PISCES

Pisces is the last sign of the zodiac. These mutable water signs are highly imaginative and deeply connected to the archetype of the dreamer. They have a romantic heart and long for an over-the-top, fairy-tale type of love. They crave romantic love the most out of all of the signs and are less concerned with hookup culture and casual dating. They are caring and sensitive in their friendships and family settings, displaying a deep empathy toward others. That said, because of their watery natures, Pisces have a tendency to become pessimistic quite fast, which leads to them acting manipulatively when they do not get their way or feel as though they have been slighted. Because they are highly adaptable, they can work in many fields—especially those that require empathy, such as social work, human resources, and sales. They are accountable for their work. Pisces also do not have a good understanding of human time, meaning they are generally running late. Due to their empathetic nature, Pisces's main lesson is to refrain from being overly trusting in all relationships—they should not give all of themselves away but rather protect their emotional energy.

YOUR ASTROLOGICAL PORTRAIT

Once you know what signs are in what planets, you can use the following chart to create an astrological portrait based on your natal chart. Note that depending on the word, a variation of it may need to be used (e.g., "reserved" versus "being reserved" or "enthusiastic" versus "enthusiast").

For example: "I am a leader. I express myself through glamour. I mask myself as a perfectionist. I communicate supportively. In love I am sensual. In combat I am harsh." This paints a larger picture than just saying "I am a leader." By looking at the various facets of your chart, you can better gauge how compatible you are with someone else.

	SUN	MOON	RISING	MERCURY	VENUS	MARS
ARIES	Leader	Ambitious	Assertive	Energetic	Bold	Fighter
TAURUS	Loyal	Indulgent	Grounded	Supportive	Sensual	Stubborn
GEMINI	Communicator	Contemplative	Expressive	Social	Poetic	Harsh
CANCER	Emotional	Intuitive	Reserved	Auditor	Lover	Temperamental
LEO	Egotistical	Powerful	Confident	Courageous	Dominating	Uncompromising
VIRGO	Organized	Perfectionist	Observant	Analytical	Teammate	Nagging
LIBRA	Diplomatic	Glamorous	Charismatic	Indecisive	Partner	Neutral
SCORPIO	Magnetic	Supernatural	Mysterious	Investigative	Erotic	Venomous
SAGITTARIUS	Philosophical	Spiritual	Enthusiastic	Intellectual	Passionate	Blunt
CAPRICORN	Hardworking	Pessimistic	Driven	Professional	Classical	Controlled
AQUARIUS	Innovative	Inquisitive	Aloof	Social	Exotic	Cold
PISCES	Artistic	Dreamer	Gentle	Empathetic	Charming	Manipulative

Understanding Compatibility

There are a few different ways to read compatibility when analyzing your natal chart compared to someone else's. Of course, the most popular method is to look at your two sun signs to determine the overall compatibility of your identities. This same approach can be used with the other signs. For example, if your moon signs are compatible, you will both operate on a similar emotional frequency, which could supersede a mismatch in sun signs. Compatible rising signs will illustrate instant attraction—or love at first sight. You can do the same with the other planets, too. When Mercury signs are aligned, you will communicate more easily. Two compatible Venus signs can showcase a positive loving relationship between the two of you. Two compatible Mars signs will show sexual compatibility in addition to a better understanding of each other during times of frustration and anger, leading to easier conflict resolution.

However, there is also compatibility in opposites. Certainly you have heard that opposites attract—resulting in the compatibility of duality. This approach is one way of interpreting yin-yang compatibility in astrology and is achieved by examining the combination of sun and moon, Venus and Mars, Mars and Mercury, and Venus and Mercury in partnerships.

Overall, when it comes to romantic partnership, the Venus sign of each person is the most important, since Venus determines what you are both looking for romantically. When one partner's Venus sign is compatible with any of the other's signs, it will denote compatibility with whatever aspect the sign falls in. For example, if your Mercury sign matches your partner's Venus sign, this shows that you both love through communication—like sense of humor. Likewise, if your Venus sign matches your partner's moon sign, you will be deeply emotionally compatible. Since Venus rules love and Mars rules sex, this compatibility is one built on sensuality. When these signs are compatible, it signifies instant attraction and infatuation that results in a powerful and passionate display of love.

Additionally, a sun and moon compatibility showcases the duality of the external and internal emotions. When your moon sign is compatible with someone else's sun sign, you will be able to understand them more on an emotional level. This form of understanding in partnerships will help the other person feel nurtured and comfortable. Likewise, their external persona will be exciting and understandable to your emotional needs.

Compatibility Chart

Considering all of the information from this chapter, you can use the following chart to gauge compatibility in relationships.

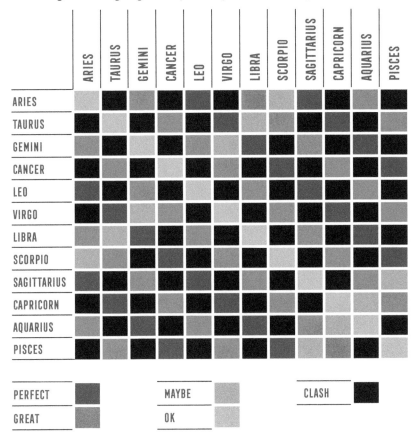

Perfect: Indicates that you are a complete astrological match! These matches all reside within the same elemental family—meaning that your energy levels and the similarity between the two of you make an excellent love match.

Great: Signifies complementary elemental signs. These are very favorable matches because while they are different energetically, they share similar energy levels, making it easy to navigate partnerships of all kinds.

Okay: Highlights same-sign compatibility. There will likely be an instant chemistry and liking between the two of you. However, your similarity can also cause frustrations.

Maybe: Showcases a ruling planet compatibility. Although these signs are very different, they are also potentially favorable, as the planetary energies that rule each sign are the same, meaning that although there will be some opposition, there is ultimately a level of deep understanding.

Clash: Details the signs in their least compatible stages. This means that you will have a hard time making a relationship progress smoothly and will need to really work on your relationship. If you clash in one area (e.g., sun sign), be sure to look at the compatibility of your other signs to see where there will be better understanding. This can help ease rocky roads.

ORBITING THE HEART OF LOVE SPELLS

When it comes to making love magic, having a grasp of astrology will help you conjure the most effective spells. Working your acts of witchery is more than sitting in your room and chanting over a lit candle—it is about having a knowledge of the natural world and how it affects mind, body, and spirit. Astrology holds a key influence over not only your emotions but the planet on which you live. On a very practical level, you can use the various astrological influences that make up your natal chart to better understand your cosmic compatibility with others—friends, family, coworkers, or lovers. You can also use astrological influences in your spellcraft to attract, heal, and empower relationships.

When casting love spells to attract someone new into your life, you could look at the signs that you are most compatible with and include those astrological symbols or overall energy types in your spells by carving them into candles, writing them as your petitions, and so on. When looking to enhance or heal existing relationships, you can use your chart and the chart of the other person to empower the areas in which you are most compatible. For instance, let's say that you and your partner are not stereotypically compatible when it comes to your sun signs, but your moon signs are complementary. You could inscribe a candle with each of your moon signs and the astrological symbol of the moon and a heart, helping to anchor your love connection through the emotional body of the moon. If by chance you are complete opposites, you can also use the charts to draw upon the opposition, asking that through your differences you may find harmony. Additionally, understanding your own astrological chart can help you learn more about your personal needs, thus further establishing self-love and self-understanding.

Having now grasped the energetic properties of the stars above, let's travel back to earth and start cooking up some love magic! Your first step—summoning self-love.

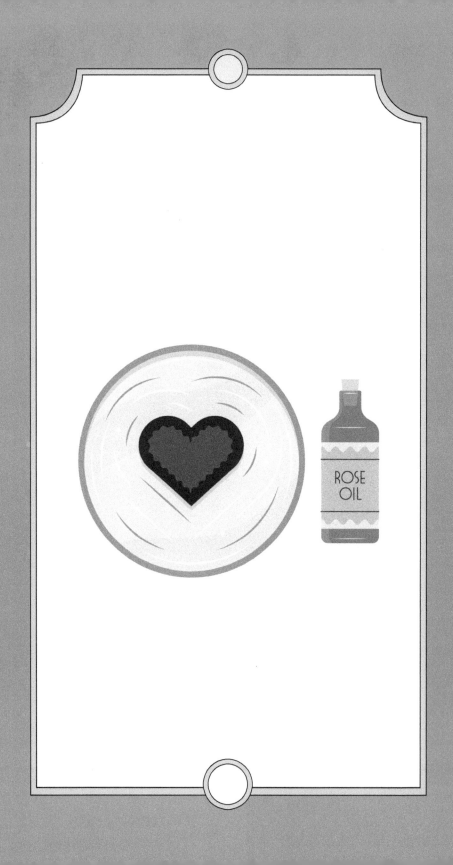

PART TWO

A Love Witch's Grimoire

Welcome to part 2 of *Love Spells for the Modern Witch*. After learning all about love, witchcraft, and the various tools and resources you can use to bewitch your love life, it is time to start spellcasting! The next section will feature a variety of spells, rituals, and potions to summon self-love from within, heal broken hearts and protect them from future heartbreak, attract new love, maintain the special spark in current partnerships, and celebrate all acts of love and pleasure. Remember that the spells are presented as suggestions to fire up the love in your life. There is no one-size-fits-all definition of a relationship. Let the spells spark the creative flame of passion within your heart. Your love, like your magic, is unique to you.

CHAPTER 4

SELF-LOVE SORCERY

To quote the fabulous RuPaul, "If you can't love yourself, how in the hell are you gonna love somebody else?" Therefore, the first category of love spells I will touch on are for self-love. When you focus on the magic of "me," you can better manifest the potent potential of "we"! These spells highlight some of the best expressions of what it means to love yourself. Loving yourself can be one of the most challenging types of love. Although you don't want to feel narcissistic or selfish, you do have to remember that at the end of the day, if you don't care for your needs, who else is going to? Look at self-love as the fuel that drives you to where you need to be. Just like a car carrying a passenger on the highway of love, you are more likely to reach the destination safely when you are fully fueled and ready to go. You cannot drive your love-mobile without gas. So get ready to pump yourself up with some self-love sorcery!

Practical Tips for Self-Love

One of the best ways to ensure success in self-love spells is to practice practical self-love. This is the magic of *do*! Let's take a look at some practical ways to anchor your magical efforts.

Treat yourself! One of the best ways to find love, romantic or otherwise, is to actively treat yourself the way you wish others treated you. This can even include taking yourself out on a date. Grab a bite to eat alone, go to the movies, walk in the park . . . anything that you could see yourself enjoying with someone else, do it alone and enjoy it.

Put yourself first. Some may think it is selfish, but caring for your needs above all else is a means for survival. You are not able to be of service and help others if you are not tending to your needs. In order to function at 100 percent, you have to recharge and refuel yourself, and sometimes that means saying "no" to that which doesn't serve you and doing what makes you happy over obligations to others.

Practice self-compassion. This is an often-neglected aspect of self-love. Self-compassion is the practice of being kind to yourself during moments of inadequacy or failure. It is okay to make mistakes, and self-compassion can help lessen the feelings of anxiety, depression, and insecurity so that you can love yourself more.

Simple Self-Love Magic

In addition to practically manifesting your self-love by working spells, let's look at some simple tips on how to actively engage in the magic of self-love.

Console your heart. A quick and easy way to love yourself when you are feeling down, stressed, or anxious is to hold your dominant hand over your heart. Close your eyes and breathe in slowly and deeply. Feel your heartbeat and the potent healing combination of touch and love.

Flower power. When you are out and about and need a boost of love, find a flower to connect with, whether it's in a park, in a store, at a reception area, or somewhere else. One of the best ways to practice self-love magic is to keep flowers in your home or on your altar to stimulate love, beauty, and self-appreciation.

Mirror magic. When passing a reflective surface, stop and take a look at yourself. Focus on what you love—inside as well as out. Compliment yourself and show appreciation for the authentic beauty you are.

Rhodochrosite Meditation

Rhodochrosite is one of my favorite crystals. It is a highly coveted, beautiful stone that does tremendous wonders in all areas of love, but particularly self-love. Rhodochrosite helps you tap into having compassion for yourself and understanding your self-worth while fully unlocking your love potential.

- Pillow or cushion
- Rose incense
- Lighter or match
- Rhodochrosite crystal

1. Sit in a comfortable position on a pillow or cushion.

2. Light the rose incense and gently fan the smoke in your direction.

3. Hold the rhodochrosite crystal in the center of your palms and kiss it gently.

4. While holding the stone, close your eyes and take 10 breaths, inhaling deeply through your nose and exhaling slowly through your mouth. With each breath, feel yourself drift further away from your mundane world and into a state of absolute bliss. Focus your mind on your breathing and how your body feels in the moment.

5. Visualize a banded pattern of red, pink, and white light softly beginning to swirl around you. As the colors encircle you in vibrancy, visualize them pouring directly into your heart.

6. Focus intently on what love means to you and how you can better love yourself unconditionally. Visualize any negativity or emotional wounds being vanquished by the rhodochrosite's loving light so that you can beam brightly with self-loving energy.

7. Visualize the colors fully absorbing into you. Once you feel you are complete, take another 10 deep, slow breaths and ease back into full alertness.

8. Carry the crystal with you for the day and repeat this meditation whenever you need to connect to your self-love.

Self-Love Bath

This is a lovely bath spell used to encourage self-love. Healing and therapeutic, it will relax your body, soften your skin, and open your heart—so that you can love the skin you are in.

- Milk
- 1 tablespoon honey
- 5 drops rose oil
- 4 pink candles
- Lighter or match
- 1 pink rose
- Large chunk rose quartz

1. Draw a warm bath. As the water fills the tub, slowly add the milk, honey, and rose oil to the water.

2. Light the pink candles and place them on the edge of the bathtub. Turn off the lights so that you are only illuminated by the candles.

3. Disrobe and stand in the tub, holding the rose. Pull the petals from the stem and sprinkle them over your head while saying:

   Flower of love, I ask of thee
   To open my heart and shower love all over me.

4. Sit in the tub and recline in a relaxed position. Take hold of the rose quartz and cup the crystal to your heart. Close your eyes and visualize a soft pink light forming around the crystal, plunging into your heart. As you glow in your self-love, reflect on what a divine expression of love your very being is. Think about all the wonderful things you enjoy about yourself and consider in what ways you can treat yourself better.

5. After about 20 to 30 minutes, drain the water from the tub and rinse yourself off.

6. Collect and dry the rose petals from the tub. Take them outside and toss them in the air as a loving act of gratitude to the universe.

Marti-Me

Cocktails and mocktails are wonderful modern-day potions that combine the herbal and energetic properties of botanical ingredients into an edible enchantment. Here is a love potion to help stimulate the self-love within.

- ◆ Chilled martini glass
- ◆ 3 ounces gin
- ◆ 2 ounces rosewater
- ◆ 1 ounce lemon juice
- ◆ 1 tablespoon honey
- ◆ Cocktail shaker
- ◆ Ice
- ◆ Lemon twist

1. Prepare for your self-love potion by placing a clean martini glass in the freezer to chill prior to mixing.

2. Combine the liquids in the cocktail shaker with ice.

3. Shake vigorously as you focus your intention of shaking up the self-love in you.

4. Pour the potion into your chilled glass.

5. Garnish with a lemon twist.

6. Raise the glass in the air and toast yourself, saying:

   I celebrate my love within and celebrate the potent power of ME!

7. Enjoy your Marti-Me and celebrate your self-love.

Mocktail Alternative

Replace the gin with soda, tonic water, or even a white tea base. If using a carbonated base, instead of using the shaker, stir the mixture in a clockwise direction to stimulate the energies of awakening self-love within you.

Cancel Comparison

The act of comparison, although so tempting and easy to do, is a venomous act that can paralyze your self-love. Comparing yourself to how others look or act and what they have (including relationships, families, etc.) does not align with self-love. This spell aims to banish the idea of comparison from your magical heart so that it can be filled with self-love.

- Knife
- Black candlestick
- 2 drops lemon oil for love cleansing
- 2 drops lavender oil for compassion
- 4 pieces rough rose quartz
- Shovel

1. Using a knife, chip away at the center of the base of the black candle until the wick is exposed.

2. Carve your name into the side of the candle. Lick your thumb and seal the carving with your saliva, locking your essence into the wax.

3. Anoint the candle with the lemon oil and lavender oil.

4. Arrange the four crystals around the base of the candle. Light the wick from the base and recite these words:

   I release the pressure that binds me
   To feelings of comparison.
   I am grateful for who I am becoming.
   No more tears will be shed as I embrace my individuality.

5. Allow the candle to burn out. Collect the crystals and any remaining wax.

6. Dig a hole in the ground someplace you do not frequently pass. Bury the remains of your spell and trace a pentagram in the soil once covered to bless your release.

The "Do You, Boo" Spell

Part of self-love is knowing your worth. This spell helps you reclaim your personal identity for *you* so that you can attract those who accept you for who you are in your life and support your true self.

- Knife
- Orange candle
- Ginger oil
- Lighter or match
- Paper and pen
- Cauldron or fireproof bowl

1. Use a knife to carve your name into the wax of the candle. Lick your thumb and seal the carving with your saliva, locking your essence into the wax.

2. Anoint the candle with the ginger oil.

3. Light the wick and gaze into the flame. Say:

   May the power of fire transpire
   The change in me I wish to see.
   May I be free to be the real me,
   Even in the face of adversity.

4. Reflect on the ways in which you love yourself. Think of your biggest accomplishments and how fabulous you are. Write these qualities on the piece of paper.

5. Fold the paper and light the corners on fire using the candle's flame, saying:

   With these words I call on the love in me
   To ebb and flow freely.

6. Place the flaming paper in the cauldron. Fan the smoke toward you so that the words from your petition envelop you.

7. Blow out the flame and dispose of the ashes outside. Repeat this spell whenever you need a dose of self-love and a reminder that you are 100 percent that witch!

Self-Love Spell Jar

For this spell, you will make a talisman with the intent of conjuring deep self-love. Once created, you can carry the jar with you as a good luck charm and to remain tapped into the energy of your self-love.

- Stick of rose incense
- Lighter or match
- Glass jar with lid
- Pink Himalayan sea salt for protection
- Pink rosebud to symbolize the heart of self-love
- Dried lavender for tranquility
- Ginger powder for confidence
- Orchid roots for grounding
- Brown sugar for sweetening
- Paper and pen
- Pink candle
- Rose quartz

1. Light the stick of rose incense and swirl it inside the glass jar to purify it with the essence of love.

2. Put the sea salt, rosebud, dried lavender, ginger powder, orchid roots, and brown sugar in the jar. As you add each ingredient, focus on your loving energy being poured back into yourself.

3. On the paper, write down everything you love about yourself. For example:

   I love myself. I love my body.
   I love my smile. I love my creativity.

4. Fold the paper so that it will easily fit into the jar.

5. Seal the jar with the lid and set the candle on top of the lid. Light the candle and focus on how you allow the wax to drop down the sides of the jar to seal it in place.

6. Top off the spent candle with the piece of rose quartz while the wax is still wet.

7. You can carry the jar with you as a self-love good luck charm or place it on your altar as a talisman for self-love. When needed, meditate while holding the jar to reinstate your promise to love yourself.

The Loving Mirror

This is a spell to rekindle the power of self-love with the power of reflection! Perform this self-love spell for seven nights in a row, leading up to a full moon.

- Rosewater face mist
- Vase
- Red rose to symbolize love
- Hand mirror

1. Before bed, mist your face with rosewater. Place the vase, rose, and mirror on your nightstand, within reach of your bed.

2. Get into bed and, once settled, pick up the rose and hold it to your heart.

3. Pick up the mirror and gaze into it as you say this charm:

   All I need is in me, and with these words may I truly see.
   In my mind and my heart may I go back to the start
   And embrace a perfect love that is all mine
   From past to present and for all time.

4. Place the rose in the vase on your nightstand.

5. Place the mirror on your nightstand so that when you wake up the next morning, you can see your reflection.

6. Do this spell every night for seven nights, leading up to the full moon. On the night of the moon, take the rose outside and place it on the ground as an offering to the universe.

Embrace Your Inner Love God/dess

A wonderful way to tap into self-love is to tap into your inner love god/dess. The goal of this ritual is to divine yourself with love's energy and emulate it with your own personal power.

- 7 white candles
- Sandalwood and rose incense
- Lighter or match
- Image of deity of choice
- 1 bouquet white roses
- Cushion or pillow
- Sparkling wine or juice
- Journal and pen (optional)

1. With the candles, create a circle large enough to move around in.

2. Light the candles and incense. Place the image of the deity and your bouquet of roses in the center of the circle, along with a cushion or pillow to sit on.

3. Close your eyes and take 10 breaths, inhaling deeply through your nose and exhaling slowly through your mouth. With each breath, feel yourself drift further away from this mundane world and into a state of relaxation outside time and place.

4. Visualize yourself glowing in a pinkish-white light as you recite these words:

   Love's divine for all time, a love that is pure and all mine.
   I conjure the love within me, my loving divinity.
   May you flow through my veins within
   And soar on the breeze all around me.
   All is full of love—my love.

5. Focus on your inner loving light pulsating and beating to the rhythm of your heart.

6. Raise a glass of sparkling wine or juice to toast your divine expression of love. Savor the taste of luxury.

7. After finishing the libation, write down any reflections you may have had during the ritual.

Solo Sex Magic

This is a template for solo sex magic with the aim of loving yourself. Here you will use the power of pleasure to amplify your self-love and bask in the bliss of your personal power.

- Music (optional)
- Red or hot pink candle
- Red sandalwood, musk, or patchouli incense
- Lighter or match
- Vanilla massage oil
- Sex toys (optional)

1. Begin by creating a sensual atmosphere in your bedroom. Dim the lights and turn on any music you like. Light the red candle and the incense with the intent of claiming your personal power with self-love. Place the candle and incense on your nightstand or someplace near your bed.

2. Relax into a comfortable position in your bed. Ground and center your energy.

3. Place a bit of the massage oil on your hands and begin to massage your body, paying close attention to how your body feels and the relaxing pleasure you are summoning.

4. Lose yourself in your personal pleasure. Incorporate any toys you wish.

5. As you reach the point of climax, shift your focus to self-love and how incredible you are.

6. At the moment of orgasm, surrender to your pleasure and claim your power.

7. Re-ground and center your energy and move forward in the blissful state of self-love that you have summoned.

Thaw an Icy Heart

It is common to put up walls as a defense mechanism—believing that you are better off alone. However, doing so only hurts you in the long run. The best way to discourage putting up walls is through self-love. Try this spell to use the power of self-love to thaw the icy walls you have built.

- Paper and pen
- Large silicone heart-shaped mold
- Feather
- Pink rose
- Water

1. On the piece of paper, write the words "I love me." Place the paper in the center of the heart mold. Add the feather to the mold to represent the weightless power of soft self-love, followed by the head of the rose to represent a fully bloomed self-loving heart.

2. Fill the mold with water and place it in the freezer for a day.

3. Once fully frozen, take the heart to a safe, undisturbed place outside. Remove the heart-shaped ice from the mold and place it on the ground while saying:

   I surrender the heaviness of my frozen heart.
   I release my heaviness to bloom in softness.
   May it thaw and beat for me once again.
   I love myself. I love me.

4. Turn around and walk away from your frozen offering. Be confident in knowing that as it melts you will feel a sense of ease as your heart begins to beat to the rhythm of self-love.

CHAPTER 5

HEALING
THE HEART

Sometimes love can be a double-edged sword: defined in one moment by an excess of joy and happiness, the next by a consuming wasteland of pain and anguish. In many ways, this chapter is about navigating the landscape of heartbreak—but not just for romantic love. Sometimes the most painful love losses you experience come from friendships. The spells in this chapter help not only ease the pain but also find support, forgiveness, and gratitude for the obstacle of pain so that it can be transmuted into a higher form of good.

Practical Tips for Healing Heartbreak

It is important for you to act practically with your magic. Therefore, learn to anchor your healing love spells with these practical self-healing tips!

Express gratitude. In order to move on, heal, and grow, you cannot continue to look back in the rearview mirror at a sad, negative, or toxic situation. Instead, you have to accept it and look at what lessons you learned in the process. It is also important to look at all the other positive things you have going on in your life and focus on your gratitude for those things—promoting positivity over negativity. By doing both, you can be thankful for the experiences while setting emotional boundaries to help minimize reoccurrence in the future.

Get away. A great way to heal is to escape from your current world and take a little vacation someplace where you can recharge and collect yourself. Doing so helps push you out of your routine and offers a new perspective for creative inspiration that will heal any blue heart.

See friends and family. Surrounding yourself with people who help lift you up is the best way to get through any time of sadness. Realign yourself with the compassion and companionship of those who care and have your back.

Simple Healing Love Magic Tips

Not all magic needs to be in spell or ritual form. Here are some quick tips and tricks on how to simply heal with magic.

Animal medicine: Spend time in nature observing animals. Meditate with, hold, or cuddle pets to bond with them on a deeper level during times of sadness.

Musical magic: Although music itself is a therapeutic element, you can use the power of intention with impactful lyrics from your favorite songs. Sing, dance, and enjoy healing music as you weave magic in accordance with the rhythm of your emotions.

Nature healing: Spending time in nature can be an extremely healing and magical process. Observe and interact with the grounding element of earth, the imaginative element of air, the passionate power of fire, and the emotional energy of water.

Shadow of Love

One part of healing yourself is tapping into your shadow self—the sub-conscious aspect of your personality that encompasses traits you have suppressed, pushed away, and ignored. Your relationships tend to mirror your shadow self. By embracing your shadow and loving it, you heal not only yourself but your relationships, too, by reaching newfound levels of intimacy. This meditative spell reflects upon aspects of your shadow and integrates it into the light.

- Black candle
- Knife
- Clary sage oil
- Rose incense
- Lighter or match
- Journal and pen

1. Carve a heart into the side of a black candle. In the middle of the heart, carve your initials.

2. Anoint the carving with clary sage oil.

3. Light the candle and incense and dim the lights so you are in the dark.

4. Close your eyes and take 10 breaths, inhaling deeply through your nose and exhaling slowly through your mouth. With each breath, feel yourself drift further away from your world and into a meditative state.

5. Reflect on your shadow—think about difficult emotions such as triggers, shame, anger, unresolved hurt, and secret desires. Ask yourself how these impact your relationships with others and how you can consciously be more observant of these emotions.

6. Sit in your thoughts for as long as you like. Record any ideas, thoughts, or visions in your journal to reflect on later.

7. Repeat as needed.

To Mend a Broken Bond

Fights and arguments can be a painful part of any relationship. These inevitable occurrences often stem from misunderstandings and an onslaught of different emotions. This spell encourages you not to break up but rather to break through the problem and heal your love together.

- ◆ Stick or branch
- ◆ Red permanent marker
- ◆ 2 strands of orchid roots
- ◆ Red candle
- ◆ Lighter or match
- ◆ Red ribbon

1. Go outside and find a large fallen stick or branch, ideally from a maple tree.

2. Break the stick into two equal halves. With a red marker, write your name on one half and your partner's name on the other. Place the broken pieces on a tabletop and touch them back together.

3. Knot the orchid roots loosely at the fracture line of the branch.

4. Light the red candle and tip it so that wax falls down onto the branch's fracture line, acting as a sealant.

5. Wrap the red ribbon around the broken branches, securing them together tightly.

6. Visualize you and your partner making amends. Continue to wrap the ribbon until there is only about an inch of length left on both sides. Knot it and say:

   We were but one and have come undone.
   May we rejoin, rebend, and rebloom, as if time has just begun.

7. Store your healing talisman in a safe place.

Summon Supportive Friendship

Friends can help you get through the roughest of times while also offering companionship to celebrate times of happiness. This spell can be used to call upon compassion within existing friendships and to act as a siren call to attract new friendships that will lift you up and support you.

- Blue candle
- Knife
- Carnation oil
- Three of Cups tarot card
- Clear quartz crystal
- Lighter or match
- Bell

1. Carve a heart into the wax of a blue candle and rub carnation oil over it.

2. Place the Three of Cups tarot card in front of the candle. This card is aligned with the harmonious flow of understanding in friendships.

3. Take hold of your quartz crystal in your hand and visualize the friendship(s) that you need most right now.

4. Light the candle and ring the bell while you say:

   Hear my call, hear this plea:
   I seek friendships in this time of vulnerability.
   Come to me with healing energy.

5. Anchor and amplify the energy of the card by placing the quartz crystal on top of it.

6. Blow out the candle and repeat this spell for the next six days.

Energetic Emancipation of a Former Love

After a breakup, an important part of healing is cleansing your space of all of your ex's energy. Neglecting to do so could cause the balance within your physical spaces to be thrown off by an ex's lingering energy. This spell will assist you in emancipating the energy of love's past and restoring healthy, cleansed energy.

- ◆ Black candle
- ◆ Lighter or match
- ◆ Cauldron or fireproof bowl
- ◆ Black garbage bag
- ◆ Palo santo
- ◆ Bouquets of lilies

1. Light a black candle in the centermost point of your home.

2. Go through your home and collect any and all photos of and love letters from your ex.

3. One by one, set each photo and letter on fire and place it in a cauldron or fireproof bowl. As they burn, recite these words:

   I release you, (name of ex), and your lingering energy.
   What is done is done, and in the past for me.
   I remove these items with no feelings of shame or guilt.
   What is done is done, no more tears shall be spilt.

4. Deep-clean your home and toss every gift, reminder, or item left behind by your former lover into black garbage bags. (The color black aids the spell's banishment power.)

5. Once you have purged the poison of your ex's energy, burn palo santo to welcome harmonious energy into your home.

6. Decorate your space with bouquets of lilies to symbolize the ending of the relationship and the beauty of your new freedom.

Finding Forgiveness

When it comes to matters of the heart, there will be misunderstandings and hurt feelings from time to time. Forgiveness helps achieve understanding and compassion in times of conflict, ultimately creating a sense of peace that helps both parties move forward. This spell is designed to resolve a conflict by calling on the healing power of forgiveness. Note that this spell will require the candle to burn completely, so be sure to research your candle burn time and carve out enough time to perform responsibly.

- White candle
- Knife
- Rosewater
- Lighter or match

1. Carve your name horizontally onto a white candle.

2. Carve the name of the person you are in conflict with vertically on top of your name.

3. Rub the candle down with rosewater.

4. Light the candle and say:

   I summon forgiveness at this time
   And ask to heal this relationship of mine.
   By the healing powers of rose and water
   And the transformative flame of desire,
   May our tensions uncross and compassion be found
   So that our love may rebound.

5. Focus on the situation and how resolution can be found.

6. Allow the candle to burn out completely. This can be done in one session or over the course of a few days. Once the candle has burned completely down, you and your partner will have made up.

Hermit Tarot Meditation

In tarot readings conducted to seek answers on love, the Hermit card can signify a time of solitude between relationships in which you heal and work on cultivating more self-love. This meditation helps encourage this process on your terms.

- ◆ Hermit tarot card
- ◆ White or blue candle
- ◆ Lavender oil
- ◆ Lighter or match
- ◆ Journal and pen

1. Sit in a comfortable position. In front of you, place the Hermit card and the candle.

2. Anoint the candle and your pulse points with lavender oil.

3. Light the candle and take a deep look at the image of the Hermit card. What symbolism is there that you relate to?

4. Close your eyes and take 10 breaths, inhaling deeply through your nose and exhaling slowly through your mouth. With each breath, feel yourself drift further away from your world and into a state of spiritual solitude. Focus your mind on the solitude of darkness and the introspective contemplation of self-awareness. Become one with the moment and draw upon the transformative nature of solitude during this time and how it creates transformation in your life now.

5. Allow your mind to wander freely in your meditative state for as long as you feel comfortable.

6. Write down any relevant experiences from the meditation in a journal to reflect on later.

Sacrifice Your Broken Heart

Sacrifice is a symbolic way to offer up one thing in exchange for another. It has often been linked in the past to obscene rituals in honor of deities for their love, protection, or overall blessing. However, sacrifice can also be a way to let go and allow healing to begin. This ritual uses a strawberry as a symbolic representation of your own heart, as well as being an organic, biodegradable substance for you to release.

- Strawberry
- 3 thorns from a red rose
- Shovel

1. Collect 3 thorns from a rose. It is best if the thorns come from a dried rose that you have saved from a former lover.

2. Focus on all your sadness that has manifested as part of your breakup. Cry—let it all out. As you do, pierce the fruit with the thorns while saying:

   From the sweetness of love's embrace
   To the torture I now must face,
   I sacrifice my broken heart
   So that I may welcome a fresh start.

3. Bury your offering. As it decays in the earth, your sadness and broken heart will ease.

"F*ck You, I'm Fabulous" Shrine

During times of heartbreak, it can be so easy for the negativity of the situation to impact your self-esteem, even unintentionally. With this ritual, reclaim your confidence by creating a personal shrine to yourself that celebrates just how fabulous you are.

- Empowering photographs, images, and other items
- Fresh orchids or light pink roses
- Candle in your favorite color
- Your favorite incense
- Lighter or match
- Mirror

1. Arrange photos of yourself from various times of your life among fresh flowers and any other items of importance in a space that you see frequently. Burn a candle and incense that you are drawn to.

2. Meditate on your memories by looking at each of your photos and other items that represent the tapestry of wonder that you are. Focus on how despite the challenges you have faced, you are a success story!

3. Place a small mirror in the center of your items and gaze into your eyes. Tell yourself that despite what or who has you down, you are fabulous. While looking deep into your eyes, say the following over and over again, until the words vibrate in your soul:

*F*ck (person's name or situation), I AM fabulous!*

4. Visit your shrine and repeat step 3 as often as needed.

I'm Not in Love Spell

This spell is for the other side of relationships that is not often talked about: falling out of love. There may come a time when you have tapped out of a relationship, and this spell will help heal the guilt of hurting someone you once loved. It is best to perform this spell during the waning moon.

- ◆ 2 lilies

1. Take the lilies to a place outside that you do not frequently cross.

2. Hold the flowers in your hands and reflect upon the love that you had and the circumstances that have led you to this moment. Focus on letting the relationship go so that both you and they can be happier. State:

   (Name), I am not in love with you anymore.
   I honor the love that we once shared,
   But I want to be free.
   As these flowers fade, I release thee.
   As these flowers fade, no more guilt shall live in me.
   With our hearts no longer bound, so shall it be.

3. Place the lilies on the ground, turn around, and walk away. As the life from the petals begins to fade and decay, so too shall the relationship—and with it the guilt that comes from letting go.

Thank You, Next!

Expressing gratitude is a wonderful way to banish bitterness and achieve self-empowerment from your past relationships. Just like the lyrical siren Ariana Grande, you will be saying, "Thank you, next!" after this contemplative and symbolic gratitude ritual. You will need one floating candle per person you wish to thank. Note that this spell will require the candles to burn completely; be sure to research your candle burn time and carve out enough time to perform responsibly.

- ◆ White floating candles (1 per person)
- ◆ Knife
- ◆ Large bowl of water
- ◆ Lighter or match

1. Carve the name or initials of each individual into the bottom of a candle.

2. Place the floating candles into the bowl of water.

3. Light one of the candles and focus on your relationship with the person—the good, bad, happy, and sad. Think about the lessons you have learned and what you are grateful for. State this out loud. Repeat this step with a new candle for each person you wish to honor.

4. While performing this ritual, focus on the symbolic representation of the water and your emotional current within. Each of the candles represents one of the people you are grateful for, and each flame represents the love that you shared. As the candles burn and fade, the water remains calm and peaceful.

5. Once all the candles have extinguished, remove any debris from the water and discard it outside in a flower garden or in the soil of plants around your home to ground your emotions and as an offering of gratitude.

CHAPTER 6

BANISHING TOXIC LOVE

In many ways, society force-feeds you the importance of being "giving" in love: In order to achieve love, you must submit to another. However, that is not the equality that is necessary when it comes to love. Nobody enjoys heartbreak, so it is important to protect your energy from the psychic vampires who lurk in the shadows, hoping to seduce you with romanticism only to later pluck out your heart. This chapter provides not only some magical means of protecting your heart, personal power, and energy from the onslaught of negativity in the world but also spells to cut ties, bring justice, and banish the hurt from those who have taken advantage of your loving heart.

Practical Tips for Protection

Protecting your heart is more than practicing spellcraft. You must anchor your efforts in the real world with practical application. To make the most of your magical efforts, be sure to use these real-world tips for protection.

Go slow. Going slow allows you and your partner to spend quality time together and authentically determine whether you are a true match. Hurried relationships of any kind often result in emotional and financial hardships.

Read the red flags. Listen to your intuition—that inner fire alarm that *ding-ding-ding*s when something is either super aligned or majorly misaligned with your energy. When people show you their true colors, you must accept them and move on in order to protect yourself. Any form of abuse, dishonesty, or mistrust must be taken as a warning sign and addressed. Do not allow yourself to be taken advantage of.

Don't be superficial. Maybe they are a total catch on paper—but the best way to live a fairy tale is to stop comparing your life to what others, including yourself, think it should be! Rather than good looks, big bank accounts, or luxury accessories, focus on someone's confidence and kindness—they go a lot further.

Simple Love-Based Protection Magic

In addition to practically manifesting your protection, here are some simple tips on how to manifest protective love magic.

Ask the cards. Do tarot readings or other forms of divination to determine if a new love (or any other relationship, for that matter) is beneficial to you. Remember that not everyone has your best interest at heart, and as witches we have ways of seeing this for what it is and dipping out of situations that do not serve us.

Reverse bad luck. The best way to undo bad luck on the go is to reverse an article of clothing. Wear your underwear or socks inside out, change up the wrist or fingers you wear your jewelry on, part your hair on the other side, and so on. Chant "reverse" over and over while reversing.

Salt protection. All witches should carry a packet of salt on them. In the event you are engaging with someone who is displaying red flags, pour the contents of the salt around you as a barrier for bullshit.

Cord Cutting

In witchcraft, cord cutting is a popular way to remove the energetic link between you and another. Especially potent when it comes to heartbreak, this spell will help dismantle the energetic bond between you and this partner.

- Red joined wick candles
- Knife
- Chili, cayenne, or black pepper oil
- Two candlestick holders
- Match

1. Gather the two candlesticks that are joined by the same wick.

2. Carve your name on one and the name of the person you are cutting cords with on the other.

3. Anoint each candle with the oil.

4. Place each candle in a holder so that the wick between them is taut.

5. Strike a match and place it slightly under the wick, not actually touching. Say:

   Our flame ignited has reached the end,
   A love that now must suspend.

6. Set the centermost point of the wick on fire and say:

   I separate the ties that bind
   And bid you farewell with peace of mind.

7. Close your eyes and visualize the person in front of you as you each turn and walk away.

8. Allow the candles to burn completely out.

Banish Toxic Patterns

It is important to learn that we must stop expecting new results from repetitive toxic behaviors. This includes the people you allow into your life. This spell uses a magical doll, or *poppet*, to represent a person and to end toxic patterns and open your heart to new possibilities.

- Black candle
- Lighter or match
- Clay
- Body bits
- Tumbled thulite
- Black cord
- 2 pins or needles

1. By the light of a black candle, mold a humanoid figure out of clay. While constructing it, add some of your body bits, such as cut hair, shavings, or nails, to seal your energy into the poppet.

2. Once the doll is formed, push the thulite crystal into its center. Kiss the doll three times and say:

   I am you and you are me, an extension of my energy.

3. Take the black cord and wrap it around the doll until it is completely covered in the binding. While doing this, chant:

   I bind myself from making bad decisions.

4. Drip the black wax onto the end of the cord to secure it in place.

5. Push one pin into the head of the doll, saying:

   I cast toxic patterns from my mind.

6. Push one pin into the heart of the doll, saying:

   I cast toxic patterns from my heart.

7. Store the poppet in a safe space. In the event you ever wish to reverse the spell, remove the pins, cut the cords, and bury the doll.

To Expose a Lie

Lies and malicious secrets are some of the most painful catalysts of heart-break. Whether you are trying to catch a cheating lover or expose the deceits of friends and family members, this cooking magic spell can be incorporated into a home-cooked meal to help cut the illusions of a liar. Be sure to invite the person you are suspicious of over for the meal and prepare before their arrival. Of course, if they are allergic to any of the items in this recipe, do not proceed with this spell.

- 1 large onion
- Knife
- Salt
- Pinch cayenne pepper powder
- Sauté pan or skillet
- Olive oil or butter

1. Slice the onion in half lengthwise.

2. Carve the name of the individual you believe is lying onto the flat side of one onion half. Carve "LIES" onto the other half.

3. Sprinkle the salt and cayenne pepper into each of the carvings. Salt is a purifying agent that also helps bring moisture from onions. Here it will bring lies to the surface. Cayenne is also purifying and assists in protection.

4. Place both halves of the onion back together.

5. Holding the onion firmly in place, begin to chop it while you say:

   May my intuition see what lies behind (name)'s trickery.
   Layer by layer, may the truth be exposed.
   Words and actions, your lies disposed.

6. Place the chopped onion in the oiled or buttered pan.

7. Sauté the onion and use it as an ingredient in a home-cooked meal that you will serve to the individual. As they digest your cooking, the truth will begin to expose itself to you.

Hex the Ex

Hexing should not be taken lightly. However, there are sincere justifications for hexing an ex, especially when dishonesty, cruelty, violence, belittling, disease, or disrespect was a result of the toxic relationship. These instances are justifiable reasons to help direct universal karma to the person who has wronged you.

- Black candle
- Lighter or match
- Photo of your ex
- Black pen or marker
- Cauldron or fireproof bowl

1. Light a black candle.

2. On the back of the photo of your ex, write a list of all the ways in which they hurt you.

3. Turn the photo over and gaze into your ex's eyes. Allow yourself to feel all the pain and anger that has manifested from the relationship. Allow yourself to relive the memories. Cry, scream, and let out all your emotions.

4. By the flame of the black candle, set the photo on fire and drop it into the cauldron while saying:

   I curse you as you deserve to be
   With magnified pain from hurting me.
   May the powers of justice be unleashed on thee.
   This is my will, so shall it be.

5. Toss the ashes in an area where your ex will cross paths with them, and rest assured that they will get what is coming to them.

Freeze the Competition

This is a spell for single witches to put the freeze on any lingering competition that may adversely jeopardize a budding romance. Some may see this as a manipulative spell, but instead of forcing a new flame to choose you, it is designed to freeze the romantic competition long enough for both of you to determine if you are interested in moving forward into a loving relationship.

- Small strip of paper
- Pen
- Whole chile pepper
- Freezer-safe bag or container
- Water

1. Write the word "COMPETITION" on a piece of paper and roll it up.

2. Slice the side of the whole chile pepper and place the rolled paper inside the slit.

3. Place the pepper and petition into the bag or container and fill it with water. Focus on the surrounding romantic competition being halted while you say:

   With harm toward none, for the good of all,
   May we have a chance to make this call
   And determine interest as potential mates.
   May competition be blocked to determine our fate.

4. Put the container in your freezer.

5. When you and your interest have decided whether to make your relationship "official," remove the spell from your freezer and discard it.

The "Ex" Files

In love, jealousy can be a major killer. One of the biggest areas of jealousy revolves around exes. The "ex" files are bound to come up at some point, and it is important to honor and respect your past as well as your new partner's. This spell helps banish negativity toward both of your exes.

- ◆ Black candle
- ◆ Knife
- ◆ Lavender oil
- ◆ Lemon oil
- ◆ Lighter or match
- ◆ White rose

1. Carve the word "EX" horizontally on opposite sides of the same candle. Cross the word by carving your name vertically over one "EX" and your partner's name over the other.

2. Anoint each carving with one drop of lavender oil and one drop of lemon oil to stimulate tranquility and purification.

3. Light the candle and surround it with the petals of a white rose, saying:

   Flame of passion, show us how.
   May we focus on the present now.
   May our minds be clear and free
   From negative thoughts of exes and jealousy.

4. Repeat nightly until the candle has diminished and the white petals have dried. Bury the remains.

Love Protection Potion

It's only going to take a few drops of this love potion to protect you from the dark side of love. Note that gin (made with juniper), elderflower, and lemon are all powerful protective agents!

- Chilled martini glass
- 1½ ounces gin
- 1½ ounces elderflower liqueur
- ½ ounce fresh lemon juice
- Cocktail shaker
- Ice
- Champagne topper
- Lemon twist (optional)

1. Prepare for your potion by placing a clean martini glass in the freezer to chill prior to mixing.

2. Combine the gin, elderflower liqueur, and lemon juice in the cocktail shaker with ice.

3. Shake vigorously as you focus your intention on all aspects of protection when it comes to your love.

4. Pour the potion into the chilled glass.

5. Top with champagne and a lemon twist if you desire.

6. Raise the glass in the air and state:

   Protect me, protect my heart, protect my love.

7. Drink your potion.

Nonalcoholic Alternative

You can easily change up this recipe by substituting the gin and elderflower liqueur with a citrusy elderflower tea and topping it off with a bit of sparkling water instead of champagne.

Protect My Power in Love

You may find yourself in relationships where you lose parts of yourself (and of your witchery) while submitting to the expectations of what your partners (and society) want you to be. This spell is designed to not only protect your *personal* power in love but also preserve your intuition, the ultimate B.S. detector. This spell calls for a very specific ingredient: a Herkimer diamond, which is known for having a "crystal memory" that can be programmed with energetic reminders to yourself.

- Herkimer diamond

1. Hold the Herkimer diamond in your hands. Close your eyes and reflect upon how talented, fabulous, and amazing you are. Think about all your achievements.

2. Visualize this energy pouring out of you and into the stone.

3. Carry the stone with you or meditate with it whenever you need a touchstone to return you to the wisdom that keeps you within yourself as opposed to losing yourself in someone else.

A Purely Casual Sex Spell

This spell promotes engaging in consensual casual sex while protecting yourself from catching feelings. In doing so you can engage in mutual pleasure without complicating the arrangement. Perform this spell whenever you are heading out to meet a consensual casual mate. Note that spellcasting does not prevent against STIs, so be sure to use proper practical protection!

- 5 black candles
- Lighter or match
- Musk or patchouli incense
- Paper and pen
- Cauldron or fireproof bowl

1. With the black candles, create a circle that is spacious enough for you to sit in the center.

2. Once seated in the center of the circle, light the candles and incense.

3. On the piece of paper, write down a dedication of your intent to engage in primal passion without catching feelings.

4. Read your commitment out loud, set the page on fire, and toss it into the cauldron while saying:

   By the power of fire, I call forth my desire:
   May potent passion come my way
   Without falling in love on this day.

5. Blow out the candles and go enjoy yourself!

LOVE WITCH TIP

If you or your mate has a penis, you can add an extra level to this sex hex by enchanting a black condom before your encounter to protect you from falling into emotional *dick*sand. For extra protection, simply hold the condom in your hands and focus on your goal while you're seated in the circle of candles.

To Reverse a Love Spell

Perhaps you have already carried out a love spell, but it didn't go the way you anticipated. If this is the case, you can reverse the magic with the following spell. As a result, you can hope to find peace of mind and cut cords with the love you inadvertently manifested.

- Red candlestick
- Knife
- Candlestick holder
- 2 lilies
- Black salt
- Lighter or match
- Shovel

1. Turn a red candlestick upside down and chip away at the base with a knife until the wick is exposed.

2. Carve a heart with a giant "X" through it into the wax.

3. Carve your initials on one side of the heart and the initials of your love on the other.

4. Place the candlestick in the holder; then place the lilies on either side of the candlestick.

5. Create a circle of salt around the candle and flowers.

6. Light the flame and say:

> *By the lighting of this flame,*
> *I declare the magic between (name)*
> *and me to no longer be.*
> *I reverse the magic of our love—I free you and*
> *you free me.*
> *It is my will—so must it be.*

7. Take hold of the candle and tip it so that wax spills onto each of the lilies. Return the candle to the holder and allow it to burn out.

8. Take the flowers outdoors. Dig a hole, place one of the lilies into the hole, and bury it.

9. Repeat step 8, burying the remaining lily in another hole far away from the first.

CHAPTER 7

LOOKING FOR LOVE AND LUST

In the modern age of Tinder, Grindr, Bumble, and other dating apps, has attracting love become an ancient artifact? Are you looking for likes more than you're looking for love? It can be hard to find the right fish in what feels like a sea of superficial, hormone-driven guppies, so this chapter will provide a series of spells and rituals to attract the love that's right for you. This doesn't necessarily mean attracting a specific person, but rather opening the floodgates of love, allowing you to experience all of its wonders. You'll also find some sexy hookup spells, too, because let's be real—witches have itches that need scratching, too!

Practical Love Attraction Tips

One of the best ways to ensure success in attraction love spells is to practice the magic of *do*! Before conjuring the love of your life, let's take a look at some practical ways to anchor your magical efforts.

Get out there. Remember that if you want to catch a whale, you have to go to where the whales live! You won't find love sitting at home on the couch binging a new season of something on Netflix. You have to go out there and get it! Make yourself available for love to find you.

Be presentable. Your body communicates more than you think. If you need proof, just google "resting bitch face"! Present yourself as you truly wish to be seen. This doesn't simply mean grooming, but rather expressing yourself with warm and open body language that makes you more appealing to others.

Look of love. One trick that I learned from my bewitching mentor, Fiona Horne, was to look at the tear duct or eyelashes of a potential mate while conversing with them in person. Your eyes will naturally dilate when focusing on something small, and dilated eyes are scientifically known to increase physical attraction in mates.

Simple Love Attraction Magic

Are you a love witch on the go? Here are some simple tips for attracting love your way.

Aesthetic attraction: If you are looking for love, infuse your fashion with the fascination of color magic. Add bits of red and pink to your wardrobe to help attract love.

Catnip charm: Catnip isn't just for cats! It is a powerful agent of love magic. Try placing a bit in your shoes to help attract love your way.

Dream lovers: For witches, dreams offer an incredible landscape of premonition. Place a piece of rose quartz under your pillow at night to dream of love. Keep a journal and pen near your bed to record any memories from your dreams that might help you on your waking love quest.

New Lovers Tarot Spread

This is a great spell to use whether you have just started dating someone or you are a love-hungry witch on the prowl. This tarot spread will provide clarity on your newly blossoming or upcoming relationship.

- ◆ Rose incense
- ◆ Red or pink candle(s)
- ◆ Lighter or match
- ◆ Deck of tarot cards

1. Create a calming and relaxing atmosphere for your love reading by lighting rose incense and red or pink candle(s).

2. Remove the Lovers card from the tarot deck and place it upright in front of you.

3. Close your eyes and shuffle the tarot deck. As you do, drift out of your current state of mind and ask the universe, ancestors, god/dess, or your version of a higher power what you need to know about love.

4. Use the following diagram to draw the new lovers spread. Interpret the cards based on their positions and the symbolism unique to your deck.

   Card 1: Your underlying wants, desires, and energy

   Card 2: Your lover's underlying wants, desires, and energy

   Card 3: Your obstacles

   Card 4: Your lover's obstacles

   Card 5: The grounding energy that anchors and stabilizes the relationship

   Card 6: The ultimate outcome and longevity of the relationship if you continue on the current path

5. Make changes to your situation and lifestyle as needed to deviate away from the undesirable results and toward the desired results.

Simply Irresistible Bath Salts

These magical bath salts are designed to enchant a bewitching bath by boosting your attractiveness and opening the roads for romantic love.

- 1½ cups pink Himalayan rock salt
- ½ cup coconut oil
- 10 drops musk oil
- 10 drops jasmine oil
- 5 drops cardamom oil
- 1 teaspoon orris root powder
- 1 teaspoon dried hibiscus flowers
- Chunk of rose quartz
- Mixing bowl
- Pink or red candles (optional)
- 16-ounce container

1. Place the salt, coconut oil, drops of fragrance oils, orris root powder, hibiscus flowers, and chunk of rose quartz into a mixing bowl.

2. Use your hands to thoroughly combine the mixture while visualizing yourself attracting potential lovers. As you do this, chant:

   Come to me, come to me, come to me.
   Love me, love me, love me.

3. Draw a warm bath and light pink or red candles in your space if you feel inclined. Add a handful of the salt to the bath.

4. Enter the water. While submerged, make clockwise swirls in the water as you continue saying the chant from step 2.

5. Store the remainder of your salts in a 16-ounce container and use again whenever you are about to hit the town for some bewitching fun!

Enchanting Love Charm

A popular method for attracting love is to enchant a piece of jewelry as a love talisman. As you wear it, it will act as a good luck charm for matters of the heart. You can select any piece of jewelry for this spell; however, it will work best if it is infused with a crystal or gemstone associated with love (see page 40). You should perform this spell on the night of a full moon.

- ◆ Rosewater
- ◆ Clear glass bowl
- ◆ Piece of jewelry

1. On the night of a full moon, pour a bit of rosewater into a clear glass bowl and place it in a safe space outside or in a window that will catch the full moon's light.

2. Once the moon has begun to shine down on the water, place the piece of jewelry into the bowl while saying:

   May the waters of love bless and empower thee to be extended unto me.

3. Lift the bowl up to the moon and say:

   Lunar light from up above, enchant this (type of jewelry) with magical love.

4. Visualize the moon's rays dipping into the bowl.

5. Put the piece of jewelry on and do not remove it until you have attracted the love that is right for you.

Come to Me Charm Bag

The "come to me" love spell is a popular witchy classic to help draw a new love to you. Rather than focusing on a specific person, this spell takes the qualities you are looking for in a person and draws them to you.

- Paper and pen
- Jasmine oil
- Red fabric drawstring bag
- High John the Conqueror root
- Orris root powder
- Dried catnip
- Dried hibiscus
- Whole vanilla bean, cut into 2 pieces
- 2 red rosebuds
- 2 orchid roots
- Tumbled rhodochrosite
- 2 heart charms
- Lodestone or a magnet

1. On the piece of paper, create a love petition by writing out all the different qualities you are looking for in a love. Also include any symbols you wish, such as astrological signs that you are most compatible with.

2. Place 2 drops of jasmine oil onto the paper and fold it in half. Insert the paper into the red bag.

3. Add the High John, orris root, catnip, hibiscus, vanilla bean, rosebuds, orchid roots, rhodochrosite, and heart charms to the bag. Kiss each ingredient three times before adding it to the bag. Lastly, kiss the lodestone three times and add it to the bag, saying:

> Come to me, come to me,
> Follow my voice.
> Come to me, come to me,
> I call on love's rejoice.
> Come to me, come to me,
> The partner of my choice.

4. Blow into the opening of the bag and seal it.

5. Dab a drop of jasmine oil on the bag and carry it on you at all times.

6. Add an additional drop of jasmine oil to the bag each week.

7. Once your lover has come to you, bury the bag.

Apple Attraction Spell

This is another form of a "come to me" love spell that aims to get you noticed and draw love to you. It is best performed on a hot summer night when possible, but regardless should be performed seven days prior to the full moon.

- 1 deep red apple
- Knife
- Piece of pink paper
- Red pen
- 2 teaspoons liquid honey
- 3 drops patchouli oil
- Red ribbon
- 2 tins whole cloves
- Shovel

1. Cut the apple horizontally to expose the hidden star. Remove the seeds. Write the qualities you are looking for in a lover on the paper; then fold it and place it in the apple. Add 5 apple seeds, the honey, and the patchouli oil on top.

2. Place the other apple half back on and fasten it in place using the red ribbon. Enchant the apple by saying:

   Plump and ready I hang in sweet delight,
   Summoning love upon this night.
   My ripe heart attracts you to me.
   Come pick my love and set me free.

3. Press the intact cloves into every inch of the apple while visualizing a nonspecific love partner entering your life. Repeat this chant over and over:

   My love is ripe, my love is ready, come to me, come to me!

4. Hang the apple in your window until the night of the full moon.

5. Take the apple outside under the enchanting lunar light and bury it in a flower garden. Alternatively, you can use a planter box on your window or balcony. Love will find you.

Dating Profile Picture Sigil

This is a spell for the tech-savvy love witch that will enhance your social media profile picture with whatever type of energy you wish to attract. For this spell, you will use a personal love sigil that will be placed on your profile picture.

- ◆ Paper and pen
- ◆ Camera or smartphone
- ◆ Digital editing software

1. First you will make a sigil, or unique symbol, that emphasizes what you are looking for. Determine what mantra best represents the love you are looking for. For example, it could be "I AM LOOKING FOR LOVE!"

2. Write your mantra on the piece of paper.

3. Cross out all the vowels of the sentence. In the example, this becomes MLKNGFRLV.

4. Remove all duplicate letters. Here the example becomes MLKNGFRV.

5. Sketch a symbol that combines all your remaining letters. My example is shown here.

6. Take a photo of your sigil.

7. Using the photo editing software of your choice, overlay the symbol on a photo of yourself that you will use on your profile. Lower the opacity of the sigil to 1 percent so that it is a very faint watermark.

8. Upload your new image. Once the photo is approved on your chosen app, close your eyes and reaffirm your sigil by chanting the mantra from step 1 several times. Repeat the mantra every time you access the app.

Sweet Seduction Oil

The next four spells can be combined into one entire night of sensual seduction with your passion partner. First up is a sweet seduction oil that combines powerful aphrodisiacal scents to entice love's desire.

- 2 drops rose oil
- 2 drops chocolate oil
- 1 drop sandalwood oil
- 1 (15-milliliter) roller ball bottle
- 1 drop cardamom oil
- Fractionated coconut oil

1. Pour the rose oil, chocolate oil, and sandalwood oil, one by one, into the roller ball bottle, focusing intently on boosting your attraction and sensual prowess.

2. Add the cardamom oil.

3. Top the mixture off by adding fractionated coconut oil until the bottle is full. Cap the roller ball bottle and shake it vigorously.

4. Apply the oil mixture to your inner wrists, behind your ears, and onto your clavicle.

LOVE WITCH TIP

You can add a few drops of this oil into an unscented body lotion for a more intense, all-over fragrance!

Glamour for Sexual Magnetism

Glamour magic is the art of creating an energetic allure by reflecting an image of yourself for others to see. It's very similar to cosplay or Halloween when you dress up as a character and become a reference to them. With this spell, you will cast a glamour by dressing with the intention of seduction before heading out to find a new lover or to entice the person you are currently seeing.

- Cinnamon incense
- Lighter or match
- Mirror
- Sexy outfit
- Sensual fragrance like Sweet Seduction Oil (page 122)

1. Lighting the incense, stand in front of the mirror skyclad and look deep into your eyes. See yourself as you want to be seen.

2. Dress yourself with intention in front of the mirror. Dab some of the oil or perfume onto the back of your ears, neck, clavicle, and wrists.

3. Fan the smoke from the incense onto yourself as you look deeply into yourself and say:

   Cinnamon smoke of sensuality,
   Awaken primal desire from inside me.
   Shape to my form for all to see
   As I reflect the desire for you to want me.

4. Continue getting ready as the incense burns.

5. Lick your finger and dip it into the ash. Mark yourself in a concealed place to further carry the essence of the energy you have conjured.

Lustini Potion

This is a love potion to inspire lust between you and a new flame. Note that the recipe yields one martini and is best enjoyed in the company of a lover. Double for best results!

- Martini glass
- 1½ ounces cinnamon whiskey
- 1 ounce damiana liqueur
- 1 ounce strawberry puree
- ½ ounce fresh lemon juice
- Cocktail shaker
- Ice
- 1 teaspoon sugar
- ¼ teaspoon cinnamon powder
- Plate
- Lemon wedge

1. Prepare for your passion potion by placing a clean martini glass in the freezer to chill prior to mixing.

2. Combine the cinnamon whiskey, damiana liqueur, strawberry puree, and lemon juice in the cocktail shaker with ice.

3. Shake vigorously as you focus on your intention of stirring up the passion between you and your mate while saying:

   Spicy and sweet, passionate potion ignite our love with fiery heat!

4. Evenly mix the sugar and cinnamon powder and place on a plate.

5. Rim the edge of your martini glass with a lemon wedge. Roll the glass in the sugar and cinnamon mixture.

6. Pour the potion into the chilled glass.

7. Raise the glass in the air and toast with your beloved.

8. Savor your Lustini while enjoying each other's company, flirting, touching, and engaging in a lust-filled night!

Nonalcoholic Alternative

You can easily change up this recipe by replacing the cinnamon whiskey with cinnamon tea and the damiana liqueur with damiana tea.

Damiana Love Bites

These delicious morsels are packed with aphrodisiacs and ingredients of love and lust to help stimulate seduction and bewitchment in you and your lover(s).

- 8 ounces semisweet or dark chocolate
- Knife
- Mixing bowl
- ¾ cup heavy cream or coconut milk
- Saucepan with cover
- 1 tablespoon dried culinary damiana
- ¼ teaspoon culinary rosewater
- Spoon
- Pinch salt (optional)
- Pinch ground cardamom (optional)
- ⅓ cup cocoa powder (optional)
- Dish (optional)
- Tray
- Parchment paper

1. Start by finely chopping your chocolate and placing it in a mixing bowl. Set aside.

2. Heat the cream on the stove in a saucepan. As it starts to boil, add the damiana. Remove from heat and let stand for 10 minutes.

3. Strain the damiana and return the liquid to heat. Bring to a simmer and pour over the chopped chocolate in the mixing bowl.

4. Stir in the rosewater and add a pinch of salt if desired. Stir quickly in a clockwise motion until the mixture is smooth. As you do this, infuse the mixture with visualizations of seduction, glamour, and passion while chanting:

   I infuse you with love and lust.

5. Cover the mixture and place it in the refrigerator until firm (at least 30 to 60 minutes, but best if left overnight).

6. Once firm, make balls from the mixture by rolling pieces using two hands.

7. If you'd like, create a mixture of cardamom and cocoa powder in a separate dish. Roll each truffle in the powder and place on a tray lined with parchment paper. Refrigerate or freeze until ready to serve.

CHAPTER 8

KEEPING THE SPARK ALIVE

Relationships take work, and sometimes they need a little boost of magic to get things "happening" again, defuse tricky situations, and even save your love. The same can be said for deep friendships and family situations as well. The more you invest in getting to know someone, the more work you have to put in to keep things going. This chapter focuses on spells to stabilize existing relationships, open the roads of communication, reignite the flames of passion, and bless the love you share for the one(s) you are with.

Practical Tips for Existing Relationships

First let's look at some practical methods for keeping up with your relationships so that you can enhance them even further.

Communication is key. Remember that communication is not just about *you* talking all the time—you must also be a listener and hear what your partner has to say. Validate their feelings in the same way you want yours validated.

Don't lose your individual shine. As partners, you need the freedom to be yourselves just as much as the conjoined unit of your union. Spend time away from each other and don't lose sight of each of your passions. Although compromise is an important aspect of a relationship, it should never come at the cost of losing your individuality. So find ways to do you . . . and your boo!

Let the small stuff go. Arguments and disagreements are a natural part of any relationship; however, you must learn to pick your battles wisely. Being selective in what problems you bring up helps ease negative energy and tension. Instead of looking at every problem as something that needs to be solved, save your energy and time for the big things that matter. Sometimes it is best to agree to disagree.

Simple Love Magic Tips

In addition to the spells and rituals that follow, here are some quick tips and tricks on using magic to keep the spark alive in your relationship.

Fivefold kiss. The fivefold kiss is a ritual blessing that involves five kisses on the body (feet, knees, womb/phallus, breast/chest, and lips) during spells and rituals in some practices and covens during rituals to honor the individual as a vessel of divinity. You can use this same approach with your lover, blessing them with your love on each kiss!

Read the stars. Refer back to chapter 3 (page 47), and draw upon the cosmic compatibility of you and those you are in relationships with. By understanding your compatibility (or even lack thereof), you are more equipped to navigate rough times.

Wash with rosewater. You can cleanse yourself and your home with cosmetic-grade rosewater to enhance the glamour of love. Add a bit to your soaps, shower gels, and even glass or floor cleaner. As you clean, focus on the vibrations of love being rejuvenated.

Stabilizing a Relationship

Stable relationships are built on love, trust, and loyalty. They should also allow for each person to thrive in their individuality while remaining true to their relationship. This spell strengthens the bond between two partners, stabilizing their love.

- 2 slices bread
- Knife
- Strawberry preserves
- 2 rose petals
- 2 basil leaves
- 2 slices red apple
- Pinch sugar
- Pinch cinnamon
- Red string or thread
- Rock
- Shovel

1. Carve a humanoid figure into each slice of bread, creating two poppets.

2. Spread strawberry preserves onto one side of each poppet.

3. Decorate each poppet as if it were to represent you and your love, placing one rose petal, one basil leaf, one slice of apple, and a pinch of cinnamon and sugar on each.

4. Push the two pieces of bread together so that the strawberry and other ingredients of each piece meet, as if you were making a sandwich.

5. Tie one end of the red string around a rock and the other around your poppets.

6. Dig a hole in a flower garden. Rock first, place the talisman into the ground while saying:

   Anchored in love, trust, and loyalty,
   Stabilize the partnership between (name of partner) and me.

7. Cover the hole. As the ingredients fertilize the earth, your relationship will grow stronger.

To Bless Your Relationship

A love blessing acts as a form of protection while also expressing gratitude for and celebrating the love that you share with someone.

- Photo of you and your love
- Red pen or marker
- Rosewater
- Picture frame
- White candle
- Lighter or match

1. Create a relaxing environment where you can celebrate yourself.

2. Using the method described on page 121, create a sigil to bless your love. Draw this on the back of a photo of you and your love that makes you happy to look at.

3. Anoint each corner of the photo with rosewater.

4. Place the photo in a frame.

5. Carve the same sigil you put on the back of the photo into the white candle and anoint the carving with rosewater. Light the wick and say:

   Empowered, protected, and enlivened with love,
   I bless the relationship between
   (name of partner) and me.

6. Burn the candle next to the photo.

7. Continue saying the blessing until the candle has burned out.

Bag of Faithfulness

"Forcing" a spouse to be faithful through spellwork can dip a bit into less-than-ethical territory. This spell, however, will help keep your partner's eyes focused on you while honoring the commitments that you have made to each other. Note that this spell can also be used on yourself to encourage your own faithfulness.

- Photo of you and your partner
- Pink or green pen/marker
- Strand of ivy
- Green jade crystal
- 2 orchid roots
- Magnet or lodestone
- Blue drawstring bag
- Pinch magnetic sand or iron filing

1. On the back of your photo, draw a claddagh symbol (see page 35). In the center of the heart, write your name horizontally and your partner's vertically over yours, creating an equal-armed cross of equality and harmony.

2. Wrap the ivy around the photo while saying:

   Vine of love, bless our union.
   Through love, friendship, and loyalty, shall there
   be fidelity.

3. Add the ivy-wrapped photo, jade, orchid roots, and magnet or lodestone to a blue drawstring bag.

4. Feed the talisman by adding a pinch of magnetic sand or iron filing to the bag.

5. Store in a safe place. Add more magnetic filing to the bag on a weekly basis to keep the spell alive.

Growing Love Spell

This spell is designed to help deepen the commitment between you and a partner so that your love can grow. Whether you are looking to move in together, get a proposal, or start a business with a family member or friend, this spell will help you and your loved one reach the next level.

- ◆ Wallet-size photo of your partner and you
- ◆ Potted pink phalaenopsis orchid with plenty of flower buds
- ◆ Tumbled emerald

1. Hold the photo of your beloved and you and kiss it three times.

2. Dig a hole in the potting soil of the pink orchid. Fold the photo and place it in the hole.

3. Hold the emerald in your hands and visualize your bond with your partner growing. Say:

   Deep green beauty from the earth, bless our love.

4. Place the emerald in the hole and cover.

5. Gently touch the budding flowers and enchant the plant, saying:

   Blooming together, faster, stronger—full of love and beauty.
   May our relationship reach new heights and ascend to the next level.

6. Place the orchid in an area where it will thrive. Visit it each day, repeating step 5 while visualizing the love that you share growing deeper and stronger, allowing you to reach the next level you seek. As you care for the orchid and it grows with love, so too shall your relationship.

House of Love

This is a spell to bless your home with the power of love and keep powerful loving emotions free-flowing in the space.

- Brown candle
- Knife
- 4 pieces of rose quartz
- Rosewater
- Lighter or match
- Shovel (optional)

1. Carve a house encased in a heart into the wax of a brown candle.

2. Lick your thumb and seal the carving with your saliva to stamp it with your essence.

3. Anoint the candle and each rose quartz with rosewater. Place the crystals around the base of the candle.

4. Light the wick and say:

    In this happy home, may (name all occupants) never feel alone.
    May love fill this space. May love here be commonplace.

5. While the candle is lit, place each crystal in the farthest corners of your house. If you own your home, you may also bury each of them at the four corners of your property.

6. Place the candle in the center of your home and continue to burn it a little each day, all the while misting the air in your home with rosewater to keep love free-flowing.

7. Replace the brown candle with another, repeating the process as often as needed.

To Open Communication

The foundation of all relationships is communication. Whether you are prone to disagreements, have hit a wall, or need a push to express your emotional or sexual needs, this spell can be used to help open the roads of communication between you and your love.

- ◆ Blue candle
- ◆ Lighter or match
- ◆ Paper
- ◆ Red pen
- ◆ Envelope
- ◆ Small feather
- ◆ Cauldron or fireproof bowl

1. Light a blue candle with the intent of opening communication between you and your partner.

2. Write a list of your needs, wants, and desires that you wish to communicate to your partner. Write down any and all areas in which you and your partner are having trouble expressing yourselves.

3. Fold the letter in half and slide it into an envelope along with a small feather, which is a symbol of communication.

4. Seal the envelope and kiss it.

5. Let the envelope catch fire by the flame of the blue candle and place it in a cauldron or fireproof bowl while saying:

> *By the power of fire,*
> *May the words of this letter transpire,*
> *May (name of partner) and I*
> *Find ways to express ourselves more freely.*

6. Once the embers have cooled to ash, toss them into the wind outside. You and your partner will find the words to express yourselves.

To Ignite Sensual Passion

This spell can be used to spice things up in your relationship and to increase passion between you. It can also be used to increase fertility or virility in your partner. Change the wording and visualization as you see fit!

- Red candle
- Knife
- Cinnamon oil
- Lighter or match
- Honey

1. Before bed on a Monday night, carve five notches down the side of a red candle. Carve the initials of you and your lover on the other side of the candle.

2. Massage a mixture of cinnamon oil and your saliva into the candle to fuel it with eroticism and your personal energy. Light the wick.

3. Take a spoonful of honey and pour half of it down the side of the candle.

4. Gaze into the flame and eat what remains of the honey on your spoon, saying:

   Honey—fill me with your sweet delight so that passion and ecstasy may take flight.
   Ignite passion between (partner's name) and me, as carnal delights are set free.

5. Visualize the warm essence of passion moving through you and focus on your desires until the flame has burned down to the first notch.

6. Blow out the flame, visualizing your goal beginning to manifest in the world. Perform steps 2 through 5 for four more nights.

Sex Magic Ritual for Couples

Working with sexual energies in a magical way can be very empowering and positively affect your life. This ritual is not only a template for performing sex magic with a loving partner but also a ritual to amplify the love between you both while celebrating the sensual union of love.

- Pillows, throws, etc.
- Playlist of sensual music (optional)
- Red candle
- 2 sticks of incense (musk or patchouli are best)
- Chalice, goblet, or glass
- Champagne, wine, or deep red juice
- Body oil
- Lighter or match

1. Create a relaxing environment filled with pillows, throws, and other objects that will help ease you and your partner's comfort during the ritual. Play sensual music to elevate the mood if you wish.

2. Set up a small altar with the red candle, incense, chalice filled with champagne, and body oil.

3. In front of the altar, stand with your partner, gazing into each other's eyes. Light each of the incense sticks and together touch your flames to the candle's wick—symbolizing the joining of two flames.

4. Begin to caress each other with the intent of love and passion.

5. Upon climax, focus your intentions on how much love you have for each other while continuously chanting:

    I love you!

6. Upon completion, collectively raise your chalice and each take a sip as a symbolic toast to the magic you have both just conjured.

Two Becomes Three:
A Throuple Spell

This spell is meant to attract a loving romantic partnership among three people rather than just the carnal passions of a three-way—though it may be modified to that if you (both) wish, using your words and intentions. Also, this spell can be done by a single person looking to enter a throuple.

- 3 red candles
- Knife
- Paper
- Pen
- Magnet or lodestone

- Herbal powder (an even powdered mixture of dried catnip, ginger, and orris root)
- Lighter or match

1. Carve your and your partner's names on two separate candles and "come to us" on the third. Draw additional symbols such as your zodiac signs or other symbols that call to you.

2. Place the candles an equal distance apart in a triangle shape.

3. Write the qualities of the individual you are both looking for on a piece of paper. Place this in the center of the candles with the magnet or lodestone on top.

4. Using the herbal powder, draw a line from one candle to the next in a clockwise direction, creating the sides of the triangle.

5. Light the candles that represent you and your partner. Taking both flames, light the third candle's wick and state:

   By the lighting of this flame, two become three,
   A loving bond between you, me, and thee.
   Come to us, we call you here,
   join our love, and settle here.

6. Let the candles burn out and actively put yourselves in a position to meet the new person.

Save Our Love Spell

Relationships can be hard work, and there are often times when you hit choppy waters. This spell acts as a means to help sweeten the sours and get you and your beloved back on the same page.

- Jar of honey with metal lid
- Spoon
- Small photo of you and your lover
- Red pen
- Rose quartz
- 2 dried rosebuds
- Pinch dried lavender
- Pinch cinnamon
- Pink candle that will fit on top of the jar's lid
- Lighter or match

1. Twist off the lid of a honey jar and eat two spoonfuls of honey, saying:

   Our love is sweet like honey.

2. On the back of your photo, use a red pen to write your intentions to save your love.

3. Place the petition in the honey jar. Add the rose quartz for emotional healing, the rosebuds to symbolize your and your partner's loving hearts, and lastly the lavender for tranquility and cinnamon for luck.

4. Place the top back onto the honey jar, with the candle on top. Light the wick and say:

   Sacred flame on this night,
   Sweeten the bond between my lover and me.
   For the good of us both, so shall it be.

5. Ground your energy. It is best to let the candle burn completely out, but if need be you can snuff it and continue lighting it each day until the candle is spent.

CHAPTER 9

CELEBRATING LOVE

From witchy holidays to marriage, divorce, and even single life, there is always a reason to celebrate when it comes to love. The happiness and joy of celebrations are ultimately fueled by the power of love. To help stoke the fires of love, this chapter features recipes for you to accessorize yourself, feed the ones you love, and practice your magic in a more personal way.

Practical Love Celebrations

The celebration of love must start on a practical level! With this in mind, here are some tips on how to celebrate love on a daily basis.

Be kind. The generosity of kindness is one of the best ways to express universal love. Hold the door open for someone, smile at strangers, remind loved ones just how important they are to you, or give a random gift—the potential for kindness is vast.

See the beauty in the world. Beauty comes in all shapes and forms: blooming flowers, the first snowfall, a raging fire. Do your best to acknowledge all of these moments—both light and dark—as expressions of universal beauty stemming from love and passion.

Live life without regrets. Being your authentic self is one of the best ways to celebrate your self-love. Tell those around you how you feel. Take chances. Seize the day and make it a day fueled by love!

Simple Love Magic Celebrations

For the love witches on the go—here are some simple forms of love magic to celebrate with!

Birthday candles. Use red or pink birthday candles on cakes or cupcakes for you or your beloved. Make a loving wish and blow—transforming the flame and carrying the magic of your desire into the atmosphere by way of smoke.

Love tips. Enchant your money and loose change with the power of love. Place it on your altar and anchor it with rose quartz crystals. Carry it with you, and when you tip those in the service industry, bestow your loving energy to them.

Valentine's Day magic. Write cards to your friends, family, and lovers expressing your gratitude for their presence in your life. Kiss each card, bestowing it with your loving essence before passing it along.

Beltane Picnic

Beltane is one of eight major Sabbats, or holy days, that are observed by Wiccans, pagans, and witches. It is a fertility festival that honors all acts of love and pleasure. This is a simple and sweet way to honor the sacred day of love, whether you are by yourself, with friends or family, or with a loving partner.

- Variety of fresh flowers and/or leafy green vines
- Crystals of love (optional; see page 40 for ideas)
- Variety of succulent fresh fruits and snacks, such as strawberries, apples, brie cheese, etc.
- Strawberry tea or juice
- Journal and pen (optional)
- Books on love, such as poetry or romance novels (optional)

1. Find a beautiful location in nature and create a circle of fresh flowers and/or crystals of love large enough to sit in.

2. While in the circle, set up a small picnic space and feast on your love-fueled snacks and libations.

3. If you are celebrating with others, share your feelings of affection with one another to celebrate your relationship. If performing solo, reflect upon your own self-love and what love means to you.

4. Spend the rest of the time in your space of love journaling or reading your favorite poems or love stories.

Love's Flower Crown

Flower crowns were popularly worn by the ancient Greeks in times of celebration. Because flowers and plants hold an abundance of love energy, they may be worn for any celebration of love!

- Variety of flowers and leafy greens that exude love (see page 37)*
- Jewelry wire
- Floral tape or glue
- Scissors
- Ribbons

1. Begin by selecting and blessing your flowers of love. Hold them in your hands and visualize them glowing with the beauty of love. Say:

   May the power of these flowers heed my desire in celebration of love.

2. Measure out the length needed for your crown by creating a circle with the wire and doubling it the desired length.

3. Wrap floral tape around the entire wire. The end result will leave the crown's base looking like a green stem.

4. Cut down the leafy greens and arrange them around the crown, securing them with either floral tape (if using real foliage) or glue (if using faux foliage).

5. Repeat step 4 to arrange the flowers.

6. Finish decorating the crown by tying decorative ribbons in different colors onto the base of the crown.

If you don't have real flowers, faux flowers can be used as an alternative. Anoint them with their corresponding oils so that they are fueled with the essence of the real plant. If you use faux flowers, you'll need a glue gun to create your flower crown.

Premarital Rite of Passage

Much like a bachelor/ette/x party is dedicated to celebrating the final moments of your single life, the following ritual may be performed anytime during the week leading up to your wedding (preferably a Friday) as a symbolic rite of passage into your life as a married person.

- Rose incense
- White candle
- Bowl of water
- Quartz crystal
- Pillow
- White kaolin clay

1. Create a circle by placing each item with its corresponding elemental coordinate: rose incense in the east for air, white candle in the south for fire, bowl of water in the west for water, and quartz crystal in the north for earth. Place a pillow in the center to comfortably sit on.

2. Disrobe. Using your hands, paint your body with the white clay—a representation of purity.

3. Moving in a clockwise circle, do the following at each cardinal direction:

   East: Welcome the dawn of something new.

   South: Call upon the energy of transformation to ease your change.

   West: Declare your self-love in the process.

   North: Declare what you are willing to let go of.

4. Stand in the center of the circle. With your arms wide open, repeat these words:

   In this moment, I am painted white, painted pure, perfect in my self-love. Betrothed to no one by the sky above and earth below and elements all around. It is now in this time I am prepared to honor love and freely give myself away to (name of fiancé/e/x) to love me as I love them.

5. Bow in gratitude of love.

6. Take a shower to remove the clay from your body.

Handfasting Cord Magic

A witch's wedding ceremony is known as a handfasting. In the ceremony, a long cord is wrapped and knotted around the couple's clasped hands as a symbolic representation of their conjoined union. In preparation for your witch wedding, the following spell details how to create your own handfasting cord to use during the ceremony. Traditionally, handfasting cords are 6 feet in length, so be sure to select spools of ribbon that will allow for this. You might need more than 6 feet of ribbon, since braiding takes up length.

- 6 spools of ribbon in any color of your choice (see page 36)
- Tassel and charms (optional)

1. Knot the spools of ribbons together and separate into two halves. These two halves will be looped around each other in a continuous braided fashion. Be sure that each half is flat.

2. Make two loops around each of your index fingers. Slide the loop on your right finger (loop one) through the loop on your left finger (loop two). Pull down on loop two so that it snugly anchors loop one in place.

3. Make a new loop from the remaining ribbon of loop two and slide loop one through it, snugly pulling down on loop one.

4. Continue this process until your entire cord is made. As you do, meditate on the love that you share with your partner and how you envision your marriage will be. It's even better if your partner assists with this and helps loop the cord a bit, too.

5. If you'd like, you can add a tassel and charms to each end of the knots for a decorative look.

Anniversary Love Letter Spell

Love letters are a staple of romanticism. And what better time to communicate your love to someone than on an anniversary? This simple and sweet spell is both a ritual of gratitude and an expression of the commitment between partners, as well as a blessing for the year ahead.

- Parchment or greeting card
- Rose oil
- Red ink
- Quill
- Envelope

1. Select a style of parchment paper or greeting card that you are drawn to.

2. Reflect upon the past year that you have spent with your partner and all the time you have spent together since the day you met, including the happiness and even the sadness that has been felt between both of you.

3. Add 3 drops of rose oil to the red ink to infuse it with the essence of love.

4. Dipping the quill into the ink, handwrite a letter expressing your love.

5. Once finished, slide the paper or card into an envelope and say:

   May these words of mine touch (name of partner) deeply,
   as our dedicated love continues to ebb and flow sweetly.

6. Kiss the letter to seal it with your loving energy and gift it to your beloved.

New Beginnings Vision Board Spell

This magical craft celebrates the new beginning of love in the face of a breakup or divorce. It uses the power of two major arcana tarot cards, the Fool and Death, along with symbolic imagery to manifest the future you wish to see.

- Photos of the Fool and Death tarot cards
- Magazines, newspapers, or other printed graphics
- Scissors
- Photo of you and your ex
- Glue
- Artboard
- Marker(s)
- Paint (optional)

1. Print your favorite depictions of the Fool and Death tarot cards—both are symbolic of endings and new beginnings.

2. Cut out or print a variety of images, letters, and words that further reflect upon the imagery of the cards, from magazines, newspapers, or the Internet.

3. Glue the photo of you and your ex to the artboard. Using a marker, write:

   From our ending, I welcome a new beginning.

4. Glue the tarot cards and your selected images to the board. Be creative and have fun while visualizing the new future you want to make for yourself.

5. Enchant your completed vision board by touching the Death card and saying:

   From the death of our love, I welcome a new path ahead.

6. Touch the Fool card and say:

   Like a fool, I now leap—so catch me, universe, and plant me where I belong.

7. Hang the finished product somewhere where you can view it each day.

Single Life Celebration

The periods between relationships can be frustrating, fueling you with feelings of loneliness and uncertainty. However, these times should be considered blessings, as they are great opportunities to focus on yourself and your needs. This spell helps empower your single status with self-confidence.

- White candle
- Lighter or match
- Libation (champagne, wine, juice, or other beverage of choice)
- White rose

1. Create a relaxing environment where you can celebrate yourself.

2. Light the white candle.

3. Sip on your libation, fully savoring the luxurious taste of your freedom by the candlelight.

4. Pick up the white rose. Hold it to your heart and enchant it by saying:

   Single and free, I celebrate the magic of me.
   Alone, but not lonely, I celebrate my status with clarity.

5. Pull the petals off the rose one by one and place them in a ring around the base of your candle.

6. Gaze into the flame's light and reflect upon how this is an opportunity for you to live life on your terms in full freedom.

7. Blow out the candle. Gather the petals from around the base and take them outside. Pour some of your libation onto the petals as an act of gratitude to the universe.

Cardamom Rose Cake

This is one of my favorite cakes, adapted from the McCormick spice recipe for a vanilla cake. Combining rosewater for love, cardamom for sensuality, and vanilla for sweetening, this is love-cooking magic at its finest.

For the cake

- 2½ cups flour
- 1 tablespoon baking powder
- 1 teaspoon salt
- 1 cup (2 sticks) butter, at room temperature
- 1 teaspoon ground cardamom

- 1½ cups granulated sugar
- 2 tablespoons vanilla extract
- 4 large eggs
- ¾ cup milk

For the frosting

- 1 cup (2 sticks) butter, at room temperature
- 1 teaspoon vanilla extract
- 1 teaspoon culinary rosewater
- Few drops pink food dye

- 1 box (16 ounces) confectioners' sugar
- 2 tablespoons milk
- Culinary rose petals (optional)

To make the cake

1. Preheat the oven to 350°F. As you make the cake, continuously focus on the power of love in regard to whom you will be serving it.

2. In a medium mixing bowl, thoroughly combine the flour, baking powder, and salt. Set aside.

3. Beat the butter in a large bowl with an electric mixer until smooth. Add the cardamom, sugar, and vanilla and continue beating until fluffy. One by one, beat in the eggs. Beat in small amounts of the flour mixture and milk interchangeably on medium-low speed until evenly mixed.

4. Grease and flour a 13-by-9-inch baking pan. Pour the cake mixture into the pan.

5. Bake for 35 to 40 minutes, or until a toothpick inserted comes out clean, and remove from the oven. Place on a wire rack to cool.

To make the frosting

6. In a large mixing bowl, combine the butter, vanilla, rosewater, and food dye and beat until fluffy.

7. Gradually add the confectioners' sugar as you continue beating. Beat in the milk until fluffy.

8. When the cake has completely cooled, frost the top of the cake with the frosting and add a sprinkle of edible rose petals for decoration (if using).

Love Candles

The following is a recipe to create your own love candles for spell and ritual use.

- Soy candle wax
- Red or pink dye
- Double boiler
- Mason jar, mold, or other container of choice
- Wick made for burning soy candles
- Wick bar

- Essential oil of choice (see page 37 to pick one based on its magical properties)
- Mortar and pestle
- Dried rose petals
- Orris root powder
- Red or pink mica (optional)

1. Determine the amount of wax to use by doubling the amount that will fit in your mold/container and melt with the dye in the double boiler.

2. Transfer the wax liquid to the mason jar, mold, or container.

3. While cooling, insert the wick to the base of the mold and use a wick bar to hold it centered as the wax cools around it.

4. As the wax cools, add drops of your chosen essential oil to the mixture. You don't want to do this while it is too hot, as the temperature can burn the fragrance and evaporate it.

5. Using a mortar and pestle, grind dried rose petals and orris root into a fine powder. When the top of the wax has cooled but remains slightly liquid, sprinkle the mixture on top of the wax so that it anchors in place. If you do this while the wax is completely liquid, it will fall to the bottom of the mold.

6. Once cooled (best left overnight, even better if in the window catching the rays of a waxing/full moon), remove the candle from mold and trim the wick. Brush with mica for a glamorous effect.

A Love Spell Soirée

On the night of a full moon, invite a group of friends over for a love spell soirée. Encourage everyone to dress in something that is glamorous and bewitchingly sensual to celebrate and work a group spell together. Before your guests arrive, be sure to create the special love punch listed here so that all can enjoy the night's festivities.

- 1 bag frozen strawberries with juice
- 1 bottle champagne
- 1 bottle red fruit juice, like cherry or pomegranate
- Punch bowl
- Variety of pillows and throws
- Ambient music
- Vase of red roses (one rose for each attendee)
- Cauldron or fireproof bowl
- Love Candles (page 154)
- Rose incense
- Paper and pen (for each attendee)
- Cardamom Rose Cake (page 152)

1. Make the love punch: Thaw a bag of frozen strawberries with juice. Put the fruit in a punch bowl and pour in the bottle of champagne (clear soda will work as a nonalcoholic alternative) and the fruit juice.

2. Create an enchanting and lush environment with pillows, fabrics, and ambient music.

3. Place a vase of red roses and a cauldron or fireproof bowl in the center of the room. Burn your love magic candles and rose incense to enhance the mood.

4. Have everyone write down something about their love and/or sex lives—what they are longing for, want to improve, or are thankful for. Take turns discussing this openly among everyone in the circle.

5. One by one, set your petitions on fire and toss them into the cauldron.

continued ▶

6. Form a circle around the cauldron and join hands. In unison, say:

> *By the power of love, may our spell be blessed.*
> *Above and below, within and without,*
> *In perfect love and perfect trust.*
> *Blessed be.*

7. Take a rose from the vase and pass it to your left, continuing until everyone has a rose as a symbol of gratitude and beauty. Have everyone pick up their glass of Love Punch and toast one another.

8. Serve everyone a slice of Cardamom Rose Cake to help ground the energy and enjoy the company of your fellow love companions for the rest of the night.

CONCLUSION

Well, you have reached the end of this book. But it should not be the end of your love magic journey. Now that you have an under-standing of love, magic, and how to successfully merge the two, you will be able to attract and empower the relationships that are right for *you*. Continue to work with the materials from this book and expand on your knowledge of love magic with the resources provided in the pages to come. Continue to cast, write, and modify spells to fit your needs—and remember that magic is fueled by your intentions and actions in the ordinary world.

Every act of love and pleasure is a divine expression and a human right. In the end, love is the cure that will help you move forward, for it is built on equality, unity, and peace. The more you embrace it, shape it, and reflect it, the more you are being of service to the world around you. Love is the greatest magic of all. Believe in it. Trust your magic and yourself. Move forward and make love.

Blessed be!

Michael

XOXO

GLOSSARY

anoint: To smear or rub oil or another liquid agent onto yourself, a ritual item, or a spell ingredient

body bits: A collection of personal items such as nails, blood, saliva, or sexual fluids used in spells to directly tie the energy to the spellcaster

divination: The magical practice of using tools such as tarot/oracle cards, crystal scrying, tea leaves, or pendulums to heighten intuition, understand past or present events, or delve deep into one's magical self

enchant: To imbue an object with energy

glamour: The magical practice of creating a visual illusion, typically aligned with beauty and seduction

ground and center: A visualization and meditative technique used to focus and align your mind, body, and spirit for magical workings

hex: A spell used to summon justice to wrongdoers and provide the practitioner with a sense of closure and relief

libation: A beverage used in a ritual or spell

petition: A wish or request that is handwritten on a piece of paper. The paper and ink colors may further align the spell with the desired outcome. It may then be burned or stuffed inside another magical object in the spell.

poppet: A type of magical doll that is used to represent a person in spells

sex magic: The magical practice of using sensuality as a form of magical fruition by harnessing energy through orgasmic release

sigil: A magical symbol imbued with power

skyclad: Naked; being clad only by the sky

talisman: A type of ornament or jewelry that is used to protect or empower a spell or person

RECOMMENDED READING

To further your studies on the red magic of love spells, check out the following books.

Bewitch a Man **by Fiona Horne**
This campy and hip book of magic helped me learn how to bewitch others as well as myself. P.S. Don't let the title fool you—anyone can use this book regardless of gender, identity, or orientation!

Bewitchments **by Edain McCoy**
This is one of my favorite love spell books. It includes advanced techniques for witchcrafting your love story.

The GLAM Witch **by Michael Herkes**
My first book! Here I go into great detail on the mythology and worship of Lilith and how to find unapologetic, radical self-love in the process.

Kitchen Witch's Book of Love and Romance **by Dawn Aurora Hunt**
For the kitchen love witches, I highly recommend this practical yet magical book all about whipping up some of the finest magical treats for you and your beloved.

Love Magic **by Lilith Dorsey**
A fantastic source on love spells by my friend and voodoo priestess Lilith Dorsey. This book covers all angles of love magic, presenting numerous ointments, candles, and gris-gris bag recipes for matters of the heart.

The Love Spell **by Phyllis Curott**
This is the erotic memoir of beloved elder witch Phyllis Curott. Filled with love, magic, and many relatable experiences, this book showcases a spiritual awakening by the power of love.

Witchcraft for Daily Self-Care by Michael Herkes
Another book of mine, this book provides a template for daily witchcraft practices that are anchored in self-care—and ultimately self-love.

The Witch's Heart by Christopher Penczak
A really insightful book on love magic that is highly recommended for the more scholarly love witches looking for traditional magical approaches when it comes to matters of the heart.

Witch Way's Book of 100 Love Spells edited by Tonya A. Brown
This is a lovely anthology of some of the best love spells that have graced the pages of *Witch Way Magazine*, including some of my first-ever published spells!

REFERENCES

Brown, Tonya A., ed. *Witch Way's Book of 100 Love Spells.*
New Orleans: Witch Way Publishing, 2021.

Chapman, Gary. *The 5 Love Languages: The Secret to Love That Lasts.* Chicago: Northfield Publishing, 2015.

Curott, Phyllis. *The Love Spell: An Erotic Memoir of Spiritual Awakening.* New York: Gotham, 2004.

Faraone, Christopher A. *Ancient Greek Love Magic.* Cambridge: Harvard University Press, 2001.

Guiley, Rosemary Ellen. *The Encyclopedia of Witches, Witchcraft and Wicca.* New York: Checkmark Books, 2008.

Herkes, Michael. *The GLAM Witch: A Magical Manifesto of Empowerment with the Great Lilithian Arcane Mysteries.*
New Orleans: Witch Way Publishing, 2019.

Herkes, Michael. *Witchcraft for Daily Self-Care: Nourishing Rituals & Spells for a More Balanced Life.* Emeryville: Rockridge Press, 2021.

Horne, Fiona. *Bewitch a Man: How to Find Him and Keep Him Under Your Spell.* New York: Simon Spotlight Entertainment, 2006.

Horne, Fiona. *Magickal Sex: A Witch's Guide to Beds, Knobs and Broomsticks.* New York: Thorsons, 2002.

Horne, Fiona. *Witch: A Magickal Journey.* New York: Thorsons, 2000.

Jarus, Owen. "Woman Seeks Man in Ancient Egyptian 'Erotic Binding Spell.'" April 3, 2020. Livescience.com/egyptian-erotic -binding-spell.html.

Kübler-Ross, Elisabeth, and David Kessler. *Life Lessons: Two Experts on Death and Dying Teach Us About the Mysteries of Life and Living.* New York: Scribner, 2014.

McCoy, Edain. *Bewitchments: Love Magick for Modern Romance.* Woodbury: Llewellyn, 2000.

Morgan, Carol. "Learn the Different Types of Love (and Better Understand Your Partner)." Lifehack.org/816195/types-of-love.

Penczak, C. *The Witch's Heart: The Magick of Perfect Love & Perfect Trust.* Woodbury: Llewellyn, 2011.

Regan, Sarah. "The 8 Types of Love + How to Know Which One You're Feeling." August 16, 2020. Mindbodygreen.com/articles /types-of-love.

Wu, Katherine. "Love, Actually: The Science Behind Lust, Attraction, and Companionship." February 14, 2017. Sitn.hms.harvard.edu /flash/2017/love-actually-science-behind-lust-attraction -companionship.

INDEX

SPELL INDEX

ACKNOWLEDGMENTS

Thank you to Callisto Media and Rockridge Press for seeing the potential of this project—specifically to Vanessa Putt and Sean Newcott for working with me again and turning a tiny vision into a big reality.

To Lucy Cavendish—for planting the seed of inspiration to write a book on love magic during our interview in 2020.

To Anna Biller—for creating *The Love Witch* and bewitching me with my favorite movie witch and archetypal femme fatale: Elaine Parks.

To Lynne Herkes—for giving me unconditional love and support.

To all of my friends who fill me with love—Christina, Yazmin, Kay, Amara, Silvester, Tania, Theresa, Kiara, Chris, Fiona, Tonya, Kiki, and Valerie.

To Madam X and everyone at the fabulous Kit Kat Lounge and Supper Club for continued support and magical martinis!

And to all of my exes—thank you, next!

ABOUT THE AUTHOR

Michael Herkes, also known as "The Glam Witch," has been a practicing modern witch for more than 20 years. He is a devotee to the goddess Lilith and focuses his practice on crystal, glamour, love, moon, and sex magic. Michael is the author of *The GLAM Witch, The Complete Book of Moon Spells*, and *Witchcraft for Daily Self-Care,* and he is a contributing writer and graphic designer for *Witch Way Magazine*. Additionally, Michael hosts "Glam Fridays" on the Witch With Me IGTV channel (@witch.with.tv), offering tips and tricks for magical makeovers. He is a professional tarot reader and nationwide speaker, having presented at festivals such as Gather the Witches, HexFest, and WitchCon, in addition to being featured in an exhibit on display at the Buckland Museum of Witchcraft in Cleveland, Ohio. He lives in Chicago. For more information and to follow Michael online, visit TheGlamWitch.com.